Seeking a Better Country

Seeking a Better Country

Studies in Hebrews 11

by

Rev. Donald MacLean

Reformation Press
2016

British Library Cataloguing in Publication Data
ISBN 978-1-872556-22-2

© Reformation Press 2016

PUBLISHED BY
Reformation Press, 11 Churchill Drive, Stornoway
Isle of Lewis, Scotland HS1 2NP

www.reformationpress.co.uk

FIRST PAPERBACK EDITION
November 2016

FIRST HARDBACK EDITION
ISBN 978-1-872556-23-9
November 2016

FIRST KINDLE EDITION
ISBN 978-1-872556-24-6
November 2016

PRINTED BY
www.lulu.com

Contents

Foreword

This volume presents a collection of sermons and addresses on Hebrews 11 which were preached by Rev Donald MacLean (1915-2010) during his forty-year ministry at St Jude's Free Presbyterian Church of Scotland, Glasgow.

Beginning in the winter of 1983 and continuing into the spring of 1984, Mr MacLean delivered a series of sermons on Hebrews 11 at St Jude's weeknight prayer meetings. This series has been held in the memory of those who heard it as being an exceptionally useful treatment of saving faith and the exercise of saving faith as demonstrated in the Old Testament saints.

The prayer meeting series extended from the first to the twenty second verse of Hebrews 11, but recordings are not available for all of the addresses. The original series has therefore been supplemented with sermons preached on the relevant verses on other occasions. The sermons are arranged in the present volume in the order of the verses in Hebrews 11, rather than in the chronological order in which they were preached. Where Mr MacLean preached on the same verses, some repetition of the material becomes apparent, but the sermons are nevertheless distinct from each other and they were preached in most cases several years apart. Some differences in style can be seen between the Lord's Day sermons and weeknight addresses, particularly in that the prayer meeting addresses are more discursive than the Sabbath sermons. Whereas Mr MacLean's habit was to arrange his material into three or four headings for Sabbath sermons, he did not explicitly give headings for the Hebrews prayer meeting series. The headings provided in this volume for the prayer meeting addresses have therefore been supplied by the publisher.

Two significant themes are apparent in this collection of sermons. One is Mr MacLean's insistence that we need to have faith if we are to be saved. There is a twin emphasis on the utter impossibility of sinners coming to faith of their own accord (hence the absolute necessity of the work of the Holy Spirit in effectual calling and regeneration) and the utter culpability of sinners who persist in unbelief and rejection of Christ. Mr MacLean continually urged his hearers to embrace Jesus Christ as he is found in the promises of God's Word. As he did so, he traced out accurately and compassionately what is experienced by souls who are effectually called by the Holy Spirit.

The second theme is what an active, living faith looks like in practice. Mr MacLean frequently refers in these sermons to 'faith in living exercise,' or the repeated and ongoing activity of the soul in coming to Christ, feeding on Christ, trusting the Word, and drawing strength and comfort from the promises of God. Faith is thus not a one-off act when the soul is first united to Christ, and neither is it good enough for believers to be lethargic or slip into apathy about the promises of God's Word. Mr MacLean took the examples of what Abel, Enoch, Noah, and the others did by faith in order to show how the faith of any believer is tested and tried and how faith continually turns to Christ.

These addresses and sermons were transcribed verbatim from the archive of Mr MacLean's audio recordings at St Jude's. The transcripts were then edited in order to make the content suitable for reading. The guiding principle in editing has been to keep as close as possible to the original wording, while making whatever concessions were necessary for the sake of the reader. These mainly involve small changes to grammar and correction of ambiguities and verbal slips, together with minor reworking of text for conciseness or clarity.

A number of conventions have been adopted in this volume. Some of the many scriptural quotations and allusions are referenced in parentheses. When verses were quoted with minor alterations to fit the context, these have been retained where appropriate rather than giving the exact quotation from the Authorised Version. In quotations from the Scottish Metrical Psalms, line breaks are denoted by a slash mark (/).

The publisher would like to acknowledge with gratitude the help of a number of individuals during the production of this volume. Thanks are due to Flora Campbell for sourcing recordings, and to Pam Bateman and Catherine Hyde for transcription. Catherine Hyde ably assisted with meticulous editing. Finally, the publisher wishes to record his gratitude to Murdo MacLean, Mr MacLean's younger son, for his encouragement to proceed with this project and for permission to use a professional photo of his father.

In issuing *Seeking a Better Country* it is the hope of the publisher that readers of Mr MacLean's sermons will benefit from them in much the same way as his original hearers did, and that the Lord would bless the truths of his Word to the hearts of many.

THE PUBLISHER
Stornoway
November 2016

1 Saving faith

HEBREWS 11:1–3

Now faith is the substance of things hoped for, the evidence of things not seen. For by it the elders obtained a good report. Through faith we understand that the worlds were framed by the word of God, so that things which are seen were not made of things which do appear.

WEDNESDAY 26TH OCTOBER 1983

IN this epistle Paul, through the direction and inspiration of the Holy Spirit, was seeking to strengthen the Hebrew Christians in the face of the many adversities that they met with, to encourage them not to draw back but to continue in the strength of God the Lord. He had been unfolding to them the great and precious privileges that they enjoyed, and that we too with them enjoy under the New Testament dispensation. And understanding these privileges, and using them in order to strengthen the soul, was intimately bound up with the grace of faith. The grace of faith is a very important grace. As long as the Lord's people are in this world they live a life of faith on the Son of God, who loved them and gave himself for them. Therefore it is very necessary for us to understand not only what the grace of faith is, but also to understand the place that the grace of faith has and the exercises that the grace of faith involves.

In this chapter the apostle goes on to speak about faith and to speak about how faith was demonstrated in the case of believers under the Old Testament dispensation. The faith that he speaks of here is the grace of saving faith, of course—that is, it is the faith that stems not from the wisdom of men but from the power of God. As the Word of God teaches us, and as the Catechism also teaches us, that faith is wrought in the soul of a sinner by effectual calling. As we are by nature, we have no such thing as saving faith. We may have such a thing as historical faith—we can believe historical events although we have not seen them. And we can believe historical events in connection with the Scripture—that there was such a person as Jesus of Nazareth, that he died on the cross of Calvary, and so on. We may believe all these things in a historical way. But that is not saving faith. And as we read often in the gospels, there was also an exercise of faith that we call the faith of miracles—that is to say, there were those who believed that the Saviour was able to perform miracles. But the faith of miracles is not saving faith. Many people had the faith of miracles who did not have the faith that is spoken of here.

How the Holy Spirit works saving faith in a soul

Therefore it is necessary for us to understand clearly that the faith that is spoken of here is the faith that is wrought in the heart of a sinner by the Holy Ghost in effectual calling or, if you like to use the expression, in regeneration. Regeneration and effectual calling are really the same thing—they are just expressions that point to two different aspects of the soul being brought alive. 'You hath he quickened, who were dead in trespasses and sins' (Ephesians 2:1) is regeneration, and effectual calling is really the experience of a soul being regenerated. We cannot have this faith unless we are born again. And this faith is the first exercise of the soul that is born again. The grace of faith is the first exercise of the soul that is quickened.

Now there is a common error in connection with faith and regeneration that is taught in our day—it was taught before our day also but very much in our day—that a person is regenerated by faith. The error is that a person believes and then he is regenerated; a person believes and then he is born again. That of course is demonstrably false, because you cannot have a soul exercising a living grace when the soul is still dead. Nevertheless that idea is very popular nowadays, and it is

11

also very deceitful. The true doctrine is that the grace of faith is wrought in the heart in effectual calling or in regeneration. And therefore we read that faith is the gift of God (Ephesians 2:8). It is not to be found in the heart of man as he is by nature. He needs a change of nature so that he can exercise the grace of faith.

Therefore faith brings before us the effectual calling of the Holy Spirit. That means the Holy Spirit blessing the Word of God to a sinner, blessing the doctrines of God's Word, then giving the soul to feel the authority of the Word of God in his or her soul's experience in such a way that, first of all, that soul comes to recognise and to feel that he or she has sinned against God. As the prodigal said, 'I have sinned against heaven, and before thee' (Luke 15:18). As David said, 'Against thee, thee only, have I sinned, / in thy sight done this ill' (Psalm 51:4). Some light is let into the soul with respect to this particular point, that the soul is sinful in the sight of God.

And secondly there is imparted to the soul a desire to be reconciled to the God against whom that soul has sinned. We see that in connection with the prodigal too. 'When he came to himself,' as the Scripture says, and when he had this confession, 'I have sinned against heaven, and before thee,' he also had this desire, 'I will arise and go to my father' (Luke 15:17–18). That was a desire that he had when he came to himself. When he realised that he was going to perish with hunger, this desire arose in his heart and mind, 'I will arise, and go to my father.' And so there is imparted to the soul a desire to be reconciled to the God against whom that soul is conscious that he or she has sinned.

Now, in the implanting of faith in the soul, the Holy Spirit teaches the soul that there is but one way of return to God. The soul in the exercise of this desire may choose other ways. Very often the soul chooses the way of its own righteousness. In other words, the soul resolves to go to God after it has prepared some ground that it is ready to think will be pleasing to God. That is, the sinner expects or thinks that he can have some righteousness of his own, something that God will be pleased with, and that is the way to return to God—he thinks the way to obtain God's favour is to have something that will be pleasing to God. Now the Holy Spirit brings the soul to recognise and to see and to understand that there is no way to return to God by that door. That door is forever closed because (as the church learns and the soul learns) all their righteousnesses are as filthy rags, and their best endeavours and their best longings and their best prayers and their best reading of God's Word—their best attending the means of grace, their best seeking to be more and more earnest and so on—by all that taken separately and all that taken together they will never open the door to God's favour. That is a door that is closed, and a door that the sinner cannot pass through by any endeavours of his or her own. And therefore the Holy Spirit brings the soul to understand that there is only one who says, 'I am the door'—the great I am that I am, the person of the Son. He is the one who has opened and consecrated the new and the living way whereby the sinner should be reconciled to God.

You see, when light from the gospel comes into the soul with regard to that particular point, the desire for reconciliation is now directed towards the person of Christ—Christ the Son of God, the one who glorified the Father on the earth and finished the work that he gave him to do, the one who was crucified, the one who died for the ungodly, the one who set aside all the claims of law and justice. The soul comes to see that this is the Saviour—and the alone Saviour—and that there is none other name given under heaven among men, whereby we must be saved but by the name Jesus. So the desire for reconciliation is pointed in this direction—it becomes a desire for Christ. A desire for Christ! The language of the soul in these circumstances is, 'Oh that I knew where I might find him!' (Job 23:3). It is the same desire as the Greeks had coming up to the feast when they asked Philip, 'Sir, we would see Jesus' (John 12:21). And this soul, who has been taught the sinfulness of sin, and the sinfulness of his own sin, and who has been taught the sinfulness of his own righteousness and his inability ever to reconcile himself to God, is now coming to the Word of God and to the throne of grace, and to the means of grace, and this desire is in his soul, 'I would see Jesus!' And that's our

13

prayer, that that soul would see Jesus, that they would find the Messiah.

Now where that desire and that longing is, then they are also taught that they are to find the Messiah in the gospel. But they have to learn—and they do learn—their own inability to see Jesus, their own inability to believe. The soul with this desire and this longing is coming to the means of grace and hearing about Christ, and hearing about the person of Christ, and hearing about the love of Christ, hearing about the efficacy of the blood of Christ—and yet he finds himself unable to trust, unable to believe in Christ! That is because this faith must be secretly wrought in the heart by the Holy Spirit. The Spirit takes of the things of Christ and reveals them to the soul through the Word of God, through the gospel. Through the soul reading the Word of God and meditating on the Word of God and hearing the gospel preached, the Spirit enlightens the understanding in the knowledge of Christ—the knowledge of Christ as the one way of salvation. And then the Spirit draws the soul into union with the person of Christ. So the sinner who could not believe before comes now to believe—he comes now to trust in Christ, he comes now to rest in Christ, and he comes to rest in Christ alone for salvation as he is revealed in the promise of the gospel. And so resting in him, so being united to him, that soul comes to be numbered among those of whom it is true that 'there is therefore now no condemnation to them which are in Christ Jesus' (Romans 8:1). Their sins, which are many, are forgiven them.

Faith is tied to the promise

That leads us to notice that faith, in its initial exercise, and faith in all its exercises, is tied to the promise. We read here about these promises, that the Old Testament believers saw them afar off and they embraced them. That is what faith is—it is an embracing of the promise, and embracing the substance that is in the promise in the gospel. The substance that is in the promise is Christ the Saviour. Christ is the one who finished the work the Father gave him to do. Christ is the one through whom the mercy of God comes to the soul. But it is important for us to recognise the fact that faith needs the promise and faith is exercised towards the promise. Therefore the apostle says here that faith is the substance (or the foundation) of the things hoped for. And faith is that which brings these things to be a foundation and a prop or an upholding of the hope of the soul. That is the nature of faith—it is the substance of the things hoped for, it is the evidence of the things which are not seen. The things which are seen are temporal, but the things which are not seen are spiritual and are eternal (2 Corinthians 4:18). These things which are not seen are in the promise, and faith, as we see here, is the evidence of the things which are not seen.

Now one way of looking at this passage and looking at faith in the light of the passage is to consider the example of a telescope. Those of you who have been at sea will appreciate the example of a telescope. Here you are at sea, and somebody reports that there is a ship over a bit. But from this distance you cannot see the ship very clearly. You cannot make out what kind of ship it is, whether it is an oil tanker or a cargo ship or a passenger ship, you cannot see what flag it is flying, until you use the telescope. The telescope has the effect that what cannot be seen with the naked eye is now brought near so that you can tell whether it is an oil tanker, or some other kind of ship, and what nation its flag belongs to. These things you see are now evidenced through the use of the telescope. The ship that couldn't be seen before is now seen clearly by the use of the telescope. Well, so it is here with respect to the grace of faith. It is the evidence—the showing forth—of things not seen.

Faith sees Christ even at a distance

Now of course there are many examples of faith—indeed, this chapter is full of them. Let us take one example, Abraham. Christ said that 'Abraham saw my day and was glad' (John 8:56). Abraham lived hundreds of years before the coming of Christ and yet he saw his day. The day of Christ to him was a reality. It was there, he believed it. He saw it. Where did he see it? He saw it in the promise. How did he see it? He saw in the telescope of faith. That day was far off from the days

15

of Abraham, yet Abraham saw that day and he was glad, and he rejoiced in it, he was assured of it, he was certain about it. It was a reality to him. There was substance in it, there was evidence in it. In the exercise of faith, 'he saw my day and was glad'.

Now take another example—the promise that is given to the people of God, 'Thine eyes shall see the king in his beauty: they shall behold the land that is very far off' (Isaiah 33:17). There is a promise—thou shalt see the king in his beauty—and faith sees what is promised. Jesus is there. He is risen again. He lived two thousand years ago but faith in that promise sees Christ, sees the king in his beauty, the king that is in heaven, the king that is the glorified redeemer, the king that is the lamb in the midst of the throne. The soul sees that. How? With the telescope of faith.

And this is what we have in the exercise of faith. The soul sees Christ in heaven. Christ in heaven is brought near to the soul and to the experience of the soul—by faith they see that Jesus is the lamb in the midst of the throne, that he is glorified, that he is the high priest at the right hand of the majesty on high. 'If any man sin,' says John, 'we have an advocate with the Father,' an advocate in the court of heaven (1 John 2:1). How do we know we have an advocate in the court of heaven? Well, it is revealed in the Word of God. But how do we enjoy it? How do we benefit by it? Through the telescope of faith. By faith we see that Jesus is the advocate, that he is the high priest. We see him there and it has an effect on our souls.

Now the person is brought to be united to Christ, and brought into an estate of grace, and they rejoice in the hope of the glory of God. Now the Lord is promising to give glory to that soul. How does the soul enjoy that promise? How does the soul taste of the fulness of that promise? By faith which is the evidence of things not seen. Although they do not see the glory now with the eye of sense, yet they see it with the eye of faith—they see the city that hath foundations, whose builder and whose maker is God (Hebrews 11:10). It is in the nature of the exercise of faith, that those things which are not seen and cannot be seen with the natural eye, or the natural under-standing, or the exercises of the natural heart, are seen in virtue of the exercise of faith by the spiritual mind, by the one who is a new crea-ture in Christ Jesus. And, you see, it is most important that those who are new creatures in Christ Jesus should be exercised in this way, in order that thereby they should hold fast their profession, and also that they should continue in their profession, so that they should be able to say, 'So henceforth we will not go back, / nor turn from thee at all: / O do thou quicken us, / and we upon thy name will call' (Psalm 80:18).

Faith looks to Christ in the midst of difficulties

But, you see, it comes to this particular matter—you have a trial, you have a difficulty, you have something that needs to be cleared up, something that you need strength for. When you think of that, then you look to the Saviour who is in heaven. You can see something of this in Mary Magdalene. When she thought of how 'they have taken away my Lord, and I know not where they have laid him', she felt that, and she felt it deeply. And when the Saviour manifested himself to her—and she was the first one to whom he made himself known after the resurrection—you remember that she made to lay hold of him. But he said, 'Touch me not,' because the communion that she was to have with Christ after the resurrection and after the ascension was to be different. When Christ was with her in the world she could see him with the eye of the body, or with the eye of sense. Now that he had finished the work the Father had given him to do, there was no need for her to see him with the eye of sense. For the time being she could hear his voice. When he said, 'Mary,' she recognised him. She said, 'Rabboni,' because she had heard that voice before. But now that had all come to an end—the Saviour was to ascend and to go up into heaven and the everlasting doors were to be opened, the doors that do last for aye, that the king of glory might come into his place. Mary, in the state she was in, would have preferred if Jesus would have stayed with her. But that wasn't the way. Now she was to have Christ with her in the exercise of faith. When the Saviour says, 'Lo, I am with you alway,' then they are looking to him, and faith is looking to him and faith is bringing him near to the soul. Or faith is so viewing him that he is near to the soul. 'Thou drewest near in the day that I called upon thee: thou didst say to my soul, Fear not' (Lamentations 3:57). It is most necessary that faith should be bringing the substance of the promise near to the soul. It is through this that is communicated by the Holy Spirit that the soul exercises faith, and it is faith that leads to the enjoyment of the substance of the promise.

And if I might just go on to this particular point—the same thing is true with regard to what I was mentioning on Sabbath evening in connection with commemoration of Christ's death. In the Lord's Supper we have things that can be seen, bread and wine, but it is faith that brings us near. The bread and wine are representing the body and the blood of Christ—they are representing, in other words, Christ and him crucified, Christ as the one who died, who paid the ransom price, for 'the Son of Man came not to be ministered unto, but to minister, and to give his life a ransom for many' (Matthew 20:28). Now, although the eye of the body sees the bread and the wine, the eye of the soul sees there Christ held forth—the Christ who was on the cross of Calvary, the Christ who was dead, and who is now alive, and alive for evermore. The soul views him by faith, and feeds on what he did and the love that he revealed and the salvation that is to be found in him. So in the exercise of faith, while the person is eating and drinking with the bodily mouth the broken bread and the poured out wine, which represent and set forth Christ and his death, faith is feeding on Christ—on the person of Christ, on the salvation that is in Christ, on the love that Christ reveals, on the grace that is in Christ, and on all that is involved in the revelation that we have of Christ in the Word of God. Those who have this faith need to have it in exercise every day and to be living a life of faith on the Son of God. Christ is the object of their faith, and although he is in heaven and although he is far off (in that sense) as to his person as the God-Man, yet nevertheless to faith, he can be near to the soul. The eye of faith is looking to him, and the mouth of faith is feeding on him, as one who is a present

Saviour—the one who says, 'Lo, I am with you alway, even unto the end of the world,' the one who says, 'I will never leave thee, nor forsake thee,' and the one who says, 'My presence shall go with thee, and I will give thee rest.'

Faith draws help from the promises of Christ

Now faith itself, of course, must feed on the Word of God and the promises of God's Word, and it is in the nature of faith to bring the substance of what is in these promises near to the soul, so that it has an effect on the soul. For instance, if I take another promise: 'My grace is sufficient for thee' (2 Corinthians 12:29). Here is the child of God confronted with a duty and deeply conscious of the need to have grace in order to fulfil this duty. And Christ promises, 'My grace is sufficient for you.' Now, faith believes that, and faith draws out of Christ according to the promise, and faith believes that grace will be imparted to the soul. 'My grace is sufficient for thee: my strength is made perfect in weakness.' There is the soul feeling his weakness, and when confronted with the particular duty the soul has to face (or it may be a trial or a difficulty), Christ is saying in the promise, 'My strength is made perfect in weakness.' Faith goes out to the promise, bringing the promise near and getting the benefit of the strength that is in the promise in the experience of the soul, so that the soul is strengthened.

And I find that when there is this duty, when the Saviour says, 'This do in remembrance of me,' it becomes a duty to the people of God in due time. Some people came to a saving knowledge of Christ, yet there was some time before they found this command becoming a burden to them. For others, it became a burden closer to when they came to the knowledge of the Saviour for the first time. But whatever was the case, this is true, that this command is to do it 'in remembrance of me'. You see, it becomes something the soul cannot get away from. No saying, 'Oh, I am unworthy and I don't feel I can face up to that duty.' That comes to an end because of this burden, 'This do in remembrance of me.' Now there have been some believers who I knew, although they are now off the earth and away, who had what, for myself, I look on as a temptation. Although this command became a burden to them and they felt it was their duty to commemorate the death of Christ, yet the time passed and they did not do it. A temptation of some kind or another prevented them doing it, and they took the idea into their head that the time was past, and that therefore it wasn't the Lord's will that they should sit at the Lord's table. That is of course a grossly mistaken view. I discussed it with them and pointed out to them that Christ says, 'As often as ye eat this bread and drink this cup, ye do shew the Lord's death till he come.' As often as ye do so. They would say, 'Well, you see, this happened, and I felt it was my duty to do so, but I let the time pass and therefore it's gone.' But there's not just one time or another time, but this is a duty laid on the people of God who have a hope that Christ has been made precious to them. And this command, 'This do in remembrance of me,' does become a burden from which they can no longer escape. And when faced with coming to the Lord's Table, this command 'This do in remembrance of me' is their duty.

But Christ does not send people to duties without supplying the grace they need. That's not the kind of master he is. When he says, 'Learn of me, for I am meek and lowly in heart,' he also says, 'and ye shall find rest unto your souls' (Matthew 11:29). When the duty is there, then the grace to perform the duty is there as well. 'My grace is sufficient for you.' Very often they feel they would like to do this in remembrance of Christ, and they feel perhaps it is their duty, but they feel so weak. They are not able to perform this duty because they are so weak. Well, Christ deals with that as well. He said, 'My strength is made perfect in weakness.' That's the nature of faith—to go out to the promise and to make the strength of Christ something that is coming near to the soul, and something the soul is participating in, and something which gives enabling grace and enabling strength.

Faith is strengthened by looking to Christ

This is where faith is so important. It is tremendously important in its exercise as it goes out to the promise. It brings what is in the promise near to the soul in its spiritual experience so that it is made a partaker of the grace, made a partaker of the strength, and receives it. As we read in Psalm 28, where it is put in such a remarkable way, as one would expect, by the psalmist, who knew and understood these spiritual exercises, 'The Lord's my strength and shield; my heart / upon him did rely.' Now that's faith! 'My heart upon him did rely.' And what happened? 'And I am helped.' I am helped, I was strengthened. And therefore he goes on to say, 'With my song I will him praise.' Why? Because 'their strength is God alone'. Now, you see that? That's what faith is—it's a heart reliance on the promise, and on Christ in the promise, and the substance that is in the promise. And where there is that heart reliance, you see what happened to the psalmist. He was helped. And he was able then to sing of this: 'And with my song I will him praise.' 'I am helped,' he said, 'hence my heart / doth joy exceedingly, / and with my song I will him praise. / Their strength is God alone.'

And this is true with regard to all the varied exercises of faith. We use the expression 'justifying faith'. This is one of the theological expressions which have come into religious language. What does it mean? Well, what is meant by the expression 'justifying faith' is that faith is the instrument through which the soul is united to Christ and is thereby justified. Christ in the gospel is set before sinners as an all-sufficient and an altogether suitable and willing Saviour, and when faith relies on that, the Saviour is brought near, to be embraced in the exercise of faith, to be enjoyed by the soul. You see, where the soul is embracing Christ, this is living the life of faith, this is living on the promise and looking for the fulfilment of the promise. Although the promise is far off in the sense that it has its own season for being fulfilled, yet faith brings it near. As I mentioned already, 'God the Lord's a sun and shield: / he'll grace and glory give.' The Lord's people are looking forward to that, but they will not enjoy it until the time comes for them to leave this world and to enter into Emmanuel's land. But as long as they are in this world they are looking above and beyond the world, and they are looking to Christ, and desiring to be with Christ, and to eventually be in glory with him. And however thin their hope may get in this world, it is relying on the promise. When faith is in living exercise, faith brings Christ near to the soul. It brings Christ, as the Lamb in the midst of the throne, and the glory that is there, near to the soul. 'Thine eyes shall see the king in his beauty: they shall behold the land that is very far off.'

By faith the elders obtained a good report

I would just like for a moment to notice what is said here, 'By it the elders obtained a good report.' The 'elders' are the Old Testament saints who are mentioned in this chapter. They are the elders, or ancients, those who were under the Old Testament dispensation. Paul says here that 'by faith the elders obtained a good report'. In the prophecy of Isaiah we read of him complaining to the Lord and saying, 'Who hath believed our report?' That 'report' is the report of the gospel. That is not the report that is meant here. The 'good report' here means that they obtained a good testimony, or that there is a good report with respect to themselves (not with respect to the gospel but with respect to them). By faith and by the possession of faith they obtained the approval of God and had a good testimony with regard to themselves.

You see this in connection with Cain and Abel. Cain brought an offering of the fruits of the ground, but Abel brought an offering of animals, and 'by faith Abel offered unto God a more excellent sacrifice than Cain, by which he obtained witness that he was righteous.' That's what the 'report' means: he 'obtained witness'. There is a good report about Abel and there's a good report about the others of whom we read here. That tells us that the Old Testament saints, like the New Testament saints, came into the approval of God. They came to be approved of by God in virtue of the exercise of faith that united them to Christ—in their case the Christ who was to come; in our case the Christ who has come. There is no other way by which we can obtain the approval of God but by faith in Jesus Christ, by our heart relying on him and on his salvation for time and for eternity, for without faith, as we read here, it is impossible to please him. Where their faith was in living exercise, and in virtue of their union to Christ, the elders obtained a good report.

By faith we understand creation by God

Then Paul goes on to demonstrate how faith acts with respect to creation. 'By faith we understand that the worlds were framed by the word of God, so that the things which are seen were not made of things which do appear.' In other words, faith believes in the revelation that God has given in his Word of the creation of the world, both with regard to what we call 'immediate creation' (that is, the forming of all things out of nothing) and 'mediate creation' (by which in the six days all the things were formed), and all by the word of God.

Now faith believes that. We were singing in Psalm 19, 'The heavens God's glory do declare, / the skies his hand-works preach.' They demonstrate and they make known the wisdom, the power and the Godhead of Jehovah, the creator of the ends of the earth, who neither faints nor is weary. And faith believes that. Faith understands it. There is a spiritual understanding of it that goes above and beyond all that we hear about nowadays with regard to the evolutionary hypothesis, which is just a mere exercise of human wisdom. The people of God believe that God is the creator. They believe that this world is his creation. They view the things that are seen—the sun, the moon and stars—and they know and they understand that beyond that is the glory of God who is from everlasting to everlasting God, whose power and whose Godhead is revealed and made known in them. In the measure in which they are enlightened they see that and they understand that and they believe that, because it's revealed in the Word of God. It's revealed in the Word of God as given to Moses, as we have it in the book of Genesis.

For all that is said, for all that people say and claim, the fact of the matter is that the person who does not believe in creation has no faith. He may think he has plenty of faith. He may think he has more faith than other people have. But where faith is, this is what Paul says: 'Through faith we understand that the worlds were framed by the word of God, so that things which are seen were not made of things which do appear.' Faith sees beyond the sun, the moon and the stars, the world and all that's found out about it by scientific investigation and the laws in connection with it. Faith does not stop at these out-ward, visible things, but faith can penetrate into this, to see the creator of the ends of the earth, who neither faints nor is weary. Faith sees the God of eternity, and the God of infinite knowledge and infinite power, and the God who, in Jesus Christ, is the God of redemption and who saves his people with an everlasting salvation.

Conclusion

How important then, beyond description, is the grace of faith! And no wonder, when it is the gift of God, when it is wrought by the third person of the Godhead in the soul of a sinner, so that a soul is relying on Christ. 'My heart upon him did rely.' That's the very essence of faith: 'My heart upon him did rely.' Faith is a relying, it is a trusting, it is a confiding, it is an abiding in Christ in the promise of the gospel. My heart, this heart of mine, is heavy—heavy with sin, heavy with a sense of sin—and sees no way of salvation anywhere else. Well, 'my heart upon him did rely'. That is faith. That is faith resting in Christ, and faith bringing Christ in the gospel near to the soul, relying on him, trusting in him. If you say about a certain person, 'He's very reliable, you can rely on him. He's very reliable and you can trust him,' you might say in other words, 'I've got faith in him, because he is reliable and because he is trustworthy.' Well, in a spiritual sense and in a much more glorious sense, so is the Lord Jesus Christ, the Saviour of the lost and undone, the tender-hearted Saviour who will not cast out those who come to him. The soul comes to this exercise: 'My heart relies upon him.' It's a heart reliance. And where that is, there is faith. And where that is, there is union to Christ. And where that is, there is eternal salvation, there is a living soul—a soul that is among the living in Jerusalem, whose feet are standing within the gates and shall be praising him to all eternity. May you and I be numbered among them!

May he bless his Word.

2 Abel

HEBREWS 11:4
By faith Abel offered unto God a more excellent sacrifice than Cain, by which he obtained witness that he was righteous, God testifying of his gifts: and by it he being dead yet speaketh.

WEDNESDAY, 2ND NOVEMBER 1983

WE have been endeavouring to examine in this epistle the various exercises of the grace of faith, and especially the necessity of faith being in exercise, so that believers might hold fast their profession of faith without wavering. In this chapter we have an account given of those in whose experience these words were fulfilled, that they were not of those who drew back unto perdition, but of them who believed to the saving of the soul. They did not cast away their confidence, but held fast the profession of their faith. The apostle begins with Abel as one of those who had the grace of faith.

Cain and Abel worshipping
We read in the book of Genesis what took place with respect to Abel and his offering, and how that offering was acceptable to God. When Cain and Abel were brought up, Abel was a keeper of sheep but Cain was a tiller of the ground. It would seem from these words they had left the family home and they had set out on what we would nowadays call their careers—one, Abel, to be a shepherd and the other, Cain, to be a farmer or a tiller of the ground. They had left the shelter of their

25

home and gone out in this way to engage themselves in these particular employments.

We would expect that they had both been taught in the house of their father with respect to the worship of God. God had indicated to Adam how he was to be worshipped, and although Adam had been driven out from the garden, a promise had been given that God would put enmity between 'thee and the woman'—that is between the serpent and the woman—'between thy seed and her seed'. 'It shall bruise thy head and thou shalt bruise his heel.' So the worship of God was set up in connection with the promise of a coming Messiah.

These two points bring before us the way in which Abel himself came to have the grace of faith, because we cannot have the grace of faith unless we have brought before us the promise of God. As I have been endeavouring to emphasise again and again, the great object of faith is the promise of God. Evidently it had been the case with Abel that he came to have faith in God's promise, that is, the promise of the seed of the woman who was to bruise the head of the serpent. There is little doubt but that both Cain and Abel would have been told what took place with respect to the fall of man. They would have been told that by Adam, in their father's house. Consequently they both knew that they belonged to a sinful race, a race which had sinned against God in their covenant head, and that they were utterly unworthy of anything else but the wages of sin, which is death. Then they would also have been taught with regard to the promise that was given in the Garden of Eden (and unfolded more and more down through the centuries) with respect to the seed of the woman, the Son of Man who was to come in the fulness of the times and who was to be manifested to destroy the works of the devil. That's what these two brothers had been taught in their father's house with regard to the being of God, with regard to God's creation, and also with regard to the promise that was given to sinful man, in the promise that was given to Eve with respect to her seed.

Cain and Abel had now left their father's house. It says 'in process of time'—that is, after the passing of days, after the passing of time.

But though they had left their father's house, neither Abel nor Cain had forgotten the worship of God. Cain, just like Abel, came with an offering to the Lord, because he had been taught this in his father's house. This is a very important point—although he did not have the faith that Abel had, nevertheless he did take part in the worship of God. He brought of the fruit of the ground, an offering unto the Lord. Now Abel, on the other hand, when he came to the worship of God, he brought of the firstlings of his flock and the fat thereof. This indicates that Abel had been spiritually taught in his soul in a way that Cain was not. As I mentioned already, Adam would have taught them about God being the creator of the ends of the earth, and it is evident that that is the view that Cain had when he came to worship God, because what he brought to God were the fruits of the ground. In other words, when he came to worship God, with the kind of faith he had—and he did not worship God without some kind of faith—the eye of his faith was on God as creator. He brought of the fruit of the ground as an offering unto the Lord.

That demonstrated that there was nothing of the *promise* in Cain's worship. The promise was not in the worship of Cain at all. And that demonstrated that the faith he had was not the faith of God's elect. It was not saving faith he had. He had just mere natural faith, believing that God was the creator. Having been trained in the worship of God he came and had his eye on God as the creator, but, as you can see, in the worship of Cain there was no question whatsoever of the promise. Cain's faith being mere natural faith had no need of the promise. He felt he was obliged in worshipping God to make an offering—that he felt, he felt it in his conscience. That is felt in the conscience of the natural man, whether he is in the Christian church or whether he is in heathendom. Even in heathendom, when they worship their gods they bring an offering, whatever kind it may be. That is because their faith is a dead faith, their faith is a useless faith, their faith is a natural faith—it's not saving faith. But Abel gave evidence of the fact that he possessed saving faith, because he felt his need of the promise.

Now wherever saving faith is, there must be and there will be a consciousness of sin, and especially in drawing near to God. Abel knew this. Not only had he been taught by Adam his father but he had been secretly and powerfully taught down in the depths of his soul by God the Holy Ghost. Through the revelation which had been given to Eve and to Adam, the Holy Ghost had taught Abel that he belonged to the fallen race of mankind and that he himself was a sinner, an unworthy sinner, a guilty sinner, a sinner who had no help of man at all. He had been taught this by the Spirit of God down in the depths of his soul, away back then at the dawning of time. How wonderful it is to think of that! Abel had a consciousness of his being a sinner, and he had a consciousness also of the promise of God—the promise of a deliverer, who was to come in God's great name, and who was to be of the seed of the woman.

We see that Abel also understood that when he came to God, he needed a sacrifice—not an offering but a sacrifice. Cain brought the offering of the fruit of the ground, but Abel brought the firstlings of his flock and the fat thereof. That was because Abel realised and understood that without the shedding of blood there is no remission of sin. He was secretly taught, down in the depths of his soul, by the Holy Spirit, that if he was to worship God, he would need a sacrifice in his worship. The light on the sacrifice he got through the promise. And by the nature of his sacrifice he manifested that he felt what David felt when he said, 'Do thou with hyssop sprinkle me; / I shall be cleansed so. / Yea, wash thou me and then I shall / be whiter than the snow' (Psalm 51:7). Abel showed that he was in possession of saving faith, and that he believed that in due time the one who would bruise the head of the serpent would also be one who would be a sacrifice for sin. Indeed that was the way in which the head of the serpent was to be bruised by the seed of the woman—in the fulness of the times he would come to be a sacrifice for sin.

So in his own way, according to the same divine teaching as in all times, but according to the measure of light and revelation that God was pleased to give up to that time, Abel had faith in Christ. Like

Abraham, who saw the day of Christ, the day of the promise, the promise of one of whom God said in another place, 'I have laid help upon one that is mighty; I have exalted one chosen out of the people,' Abel in his own way understood that. He grasped this, that the head of the serpent was to be bruised by this one who was to come in the fulness of the times, and who was to die and pay the ransom price for sin, and who was to provide salvation for the very chief of sinners. The faith of Abel went out to this glorious person in the promise of God. His soul closed in with God's way of salvation, and he evidenced that by the sacrifice that he offered up.

And wherever saving faith is, that is the nature of it—it looks to Christ in the promise. Abel was looking forward to the Christ who was to come, but in these New Testament times we look back to the Christ who has come. We look to the Christ who has come in fulfilment of the promise, who has wrought out salvation, who died and who rose again and who is alive, and alive for evermore. When faith is wrought in the heart by the Holy Spirit and the sinner is made conscious of his sins, he looks by faith to Christ to deliver him and Christ to cover his sins through the merit of his blood and to be saved in him with an everlasting salvation.

The Lord had respect to Abel

Now, the next thing to notice is that 'the Lord had respect unto Abel and to his offering: but unto Cain and to his offering he had not respect.' Now, you see how it is put here, that God had respect to Abel—that's to the person of Abel—and his offering, but to the person of Cain and to his offering he did not have respect. That teaches us that before a sacrifice or an offering to God can be acceptable, the person must be acceptable. God had respect not only to the sacrifice of Abel but to the person of Abel, and he had respect to the person of Abel because of his faith.

You see, by virtue of his faith, in virtue of his being united to Christ, Abel was justified. He was righteous in the sight of God with the righteousness of Christ imputed to him. Although that righteousness had not yet been wrought out and finished on the cross of

Calvary, nevertheless, as Abraham believed God and it was counted to him for righteousness (that is to say, he believed in Christ and the righteousness of Christ, and the righteousness of Christ was imputed to him, and therefore he was accepted in the beloved) so it was true of Abel, that he was accepted in the beloved. By virtue of his faith in Christ and his union to Christ, Abel was accepted in the beloved. That must be true of us if we are to serve God in any way, or if we are truly to worship God. If we are truly to have acts of worship it is essential that we should have faith in the Lord and Saviour Jesus Christ. Before our worship can be acceptable to God we ourselves must be accepted in the beloved. That is very important. That is why the Saviour is the Mediator between God and man, so that souls can come to worship God, those souls who are of the circumcision, who worship God in the Spirit, who rejoice in Christ Jesus, and who have no confidence in the flesh. They rejoice in Christ because through him they have access to the Father, and through him they are reconciled to the Father, and through him they are accepted. They are accepted in the beloved and their acts of worship are also accepted in the beloved. This was true of Abel on this occasion, and it is something that we must remember for ourselves.

Abel's faith had respect to the worship of God, both with respect to the promise and also with respect to the form of that worship—that there would need to be a sacrifice. He had been taught all that, and his faith was exercised with respect to it. All the Lord's people are now priests—'an holy priesthood, to offer up spiritual sacrifices, acceptable to God by Jesus Christ'. They offer spiritual sacrifices—no longer lambs and bullocks and goats or animals of any kind—all that is over and done with, the Old Testament dispensation is gone. The sacrifices which are now offered by the people of God are spiritual sacrifices, offered up through the divine Redeemer, who came in God's great name to save. This is the spiritual priesthood that is spoken of in the Word of God: 'Ye are a chosen generation, a royal priesthood, an holy nation, a peculiar people; that ye should shew forth the praises of him who hath called you out of darkness into his marvellous light' (1 Peter

2:9). As a royal priesthood they offer up spiritual sacrifices to God. This is what constitutes the priesthood—by faith of the operation of God they are united to Christ and through him they offer up these sacrifices to God and they are accepted in him.

The same thing is true with regard to every form of serving Christ. As a congregation we are coming near to a particular service to the Saviour in the providence of God, and that is to commemorate the death of Christ. The first thing with regard to that is that we should be, as to our persons, in a position to render this form of service to God, and to Christ who says, 'This do in remembrance of me.' It is essential that our persons be accepted—it is essential that we should have faith in Christ and that we should be united to Christ by faith. It is in connection with that, that the people of God render this service to him. In coming to the Lord's Table they are looking to Christ as the one who has been made precious to them (and to you that believe, he is precious) in the promise of the everlasting gospel—precious in his person as the Son of God in our nature, precious in his person as the Redeemer of God's people who has paid the great ransom price for sin, and now precious as the one who says to the soul, 'This do in remembrance of me.' If the service is to be accepted in the beloved then the person must be accepted in the beloved beforehand. That's what we have here. God had respect unto Abel and to his offering— not merely to the offering of Abel, but to Abel and to his offering. To Cain and his offering he did not have respect. He didn't have respect to Cain and his offering because Cain was destitute of saving faith.

Abel offered a more excellent sacrifice than Cain

The apostle says that 'by faith Abel offered unto God a more excellent sacrifice than Cain.' It was more excellent—that is, because he had faith and because the light that was in his faith was looking to the promise, and the light that was in his faith felt his need of blood in his sacrifice to cleanse from sin. 'By which he obtained witness that he was righteous.' He was righteous through faith in Christ.

We are not told in Genesis how God had made evident his respect to the offering of Abel in contradistinction to the offering of Cain, but it is clear that it was not a secret thing but an open thing, because Cain's face fell. He realised that he was rejected. If we look at the rest of Scripture we come to the conclusion that God must have shown his respect to Abel and to his offering by fire falling on the offering and consuming it. As you remember, that's what happened on Mount Carmel with Elijah—God answered by fire. And personally I have no doubt that that is what happened here, that fire from heaven descended on the sacrifice of Abel, in the presence of Cain, when they were worshipping God (for they were worshipping together, as far as we can see). Cain knew when that fire fell from heaven and devoured the sacrifice of Abel, that God was accepting Abel's sacrifice, and that acceptance by God was testifying to the fact that Abel was righteous. Now of course that does not happen now, for those days are over. God does not answer by fire in this particular way, but he does make it clear in his Word that service to him that is going to be acceptable involves first of all the person being accepted through Christ, and also the service being rendered through Christ and in the strength of the Holy Spirit.

Now we see that when this distinction was made by God in respect of the worship of these two men, that part of the promise was fulfilled, 'I will put enmity between thee and the woman, and between thy seed and her seed.' That's what was said to the serpent, and here was this enmity rising up in Cain. 'Cain talked with Abel his brother: and it came to pass, when they were in the field, that Cain rose up against Abel his brother, and slew him.' Abel became the first martyr in the church of God, and he became the first martyr in the church of God with respect to worship, and serving God, and the proper way of serving God. This enmity goes right on down through the years. After all, was this not the contest between the Saviour and the Pharisees? They thought they were worshipping God with the kind of sacrifices that they had, but they had no faith. They were blind leaders of the blind—they had no faith. They were not worshipping God in the Spirit, and when the Saviour exposed all that, he was making it perfectly plain that it would not weigh with God. It would not be acceptable to God. As had been said by David long ago, the stone which the builders rejected was made the head of the corner. As long as they were rejecting Christ they could not worship God, they could not serve God in worshipping him. This is the great contest down to the present day. Nothing can stir up enmity in people's hearts more than when they feel the hopes they entertained with respect to their being accepted by God being swept away from them, although they have no faith and although they have no respect to the way in which God is to be worshipped. But faith will have great respect to God's appointed way of worship. It is not just a matter of tradition, or a matter of having been brought up in a particular way, in Scotland or England or America. It is a question of faith, the exercise of a living faith, the faith that is of the operation of God. And where that is, there will be a witness on the side of the truth, on the side of the Word of God. So we read in Hebrews concerning Abel that 'he being dead yet speaketh'.

He being dead yet speaketh

There are two ways at least of looking at these words, 'he being dead yet speaketh.' The first way would be that the blood of Abel had a voice, a voice to God in heaven. It was innocent blood that was shed, and the sin of murder committed, and that blood of Abel had a voice in heaven. It is also a voice to us in the records of God's Word testifying to the fact that wherever a murder may happen and however the murderer may escape the justice of men and whatever excuses may be offered for them, they will not escape the just judgment of God.

But then the second way in which we may look at this is that Abel is a witness speaking of the necessity that his person would be accepted by God. Although he was a sinner, and knew himself to be a sinner, and was no doubt very often saying, as the publican, 'God be merciful to me a sinner,' yet at the same time he was looking to Christ and looking to be accepted in the beloved, and Christ was all his salvation and all his desire. If a person is accepted in Christ, then his or her efforts at serving God are acceptable to God in Christ, however weak they may be and however poor they may seem to himself or herself.

This is also true, as I have been saying, with regard to commemorating the death of the Saviour. Some among the Lord's people may feel how much they lack the spirituality of mind they would like to have, and the spiritual exercise of mind they would like to have. Nevertheless the eye of their faith is to Christ, and when their faith is taught that they are accepted in him and clothed with his righteousness, then, when they endeavour to keep this command, Christ is saying to them, 'My grace is sufficient for you, for my strength is made perfect in weakness.' It is a mark of the Lord's people that they would desire to commemorate the death of Christ in the strength of grace, and they would desire to do it with the hope and expectation that they themselves and their service would be accepted in the beloved. They feel their need of the blood being sprinkled on their persons and on their service—they need that—nevertheless this is still speaking to us, how God accepted this man Abel, and how he accepted the offering of Abel and how he had no respect to the offering of Cain. This should be our desire, that we would be like Abel.

Yet we must understand that if we are going to be like Abel, that incurs the enmity of the world. It especially incurs the enmity of false religions who want to worship God in some other way, and who want to be pleased with themselves, as Cain was—after all, look at the time he spent in tilling the ground and all his hard work! Now he was coming with these efforts to worship God in this way, but it would not do. Abel lost his life over this controversy in the field, over the way of worshipping God—the way in which a sinner is accepted in Christ, and the way which a sinner truly worships God. If we are to be like Abel, and have saving faith, and the obedience of faith, and a delight in the worship of God, then we must expect that we too will encounter the enmity of the world. We need not expect anything else and we should not be discouraged on that account, any more than Abel was. Though he was threatened with the enmity of Cain, yet he was not prepared to let go his profession of faith. He was not prepared to let go his profession, but he kept his confidence to the end, and is now here enrolled in the Word of God as one who suffered unto death, out of his faith in Christ and the love by which faith works (for as we read, 'faith worketh by love').

That love was in Abel's soul away back then just after the dawning of time—we do not know how long it was after the creation, but how wonderful it is to think of Abel there in the light of the promise, and how he was able to discern by divine teaching the preciousness of Christ! And here we are with the full revelation. How great the benefit is!—the full revelation of the love of the divine Redeemer! How willing we should be in the exercise of faith to embrace Christ, and how willing we should be to give the obedience of faith in serving him in our day and generation!

May he bless his Word.

3 Enoch

HEBREWS 11:5–6

By faith Enoch was translated that he should not see death; and was not found, because God had translated him: for before his translation he had this testimony, that he pleased God. But without faith it is impossible to please him: for he that cometh to God must believe that he is, and that he is a rewarder of them that diligently seek him.

WEDNESDAY, 16TH NOVEMBER 1983

THIS chapter gives an account of various notable believers in the Old Testament. They were noted for their exercise of faith, that faith without which it is impossible to please God. I made some comments already on Abel and the manifestation he gave that he had faith, by offering the sacrifice he did. We also noticed that God testified his approval of the sacrifice which Abel offered up. While we are not expressly told the particular way in which God manifested his acceptance of Abel's sacrifice, it is likely, in the light of other places in Scripture, that the way in which God may have done this was in 'answering by fire'. Now we have the next case—Paul mentions Enoch. The faith of Enoch was also pleasing to God, and God on this occasion manifested his pleasure in a still more remarkable way—he translated Enoch from time to eternity so that he was 'not found'. Enoch was removed from the earth—he was not found, because he had been taken away to heaven.

He that cometh to God must believe that he is

Now we see that it was on account of his faith that Enoch received the testimony that he did. And Paul goes on to mention, in connection with this, that without faith it is impossible to please God. It is impossible to please God without the grace of faith. Paul then goes on to point out the evidence that indicates that it is impossible to please God without faith, that 'he that cometh to God must believe that he is.' That is absolutely essential for a true coming to God, and a true coming to God in order to be accepted by him. In coming to God we must believe that he is, and believe that he is the glorious being that he reveals himself in his Word to be.

As we are by nature, we do not believe that God is who he declares himself to be. We may believe that there is a God—indeed it is left in the conscience of men even after the fall, that they have a sense of the fact that there is a God. That is the foundation of all the religions of every description and kind that are in the world. It is because of that sense of deity, that sense in the soul of man that there is a God. All the idolatrous religions and every form of religion that is in the world arises out of the sense in the soul of man that there is a God. But as we read in the Acts of the Apostles, although the Athenians had an altar (so they believed there was a God), yet it was an altar to an unknown God, a God they did not know. But the grace of faith means that we believe that God is. Where there is saving faith in the soul, then there is the belief that God is. That involves believing that he is who he reveals himself to be. He makes himself known as the God who is holy and just and true, the God in whose sight sin is an abominable thing which he hates, and he makes known that it is impossible for us, as we are in ourselves, for us to please God as we are, whatever we may endeavour to do. Just as Cain came with his own sacrifice, and thought, no doubt, that God should be well pleased with it, so we too are apt to think that God ought to be pleased with the things that we do in religion. But the fact is that, as long as our sins are unforgiven and as long as we are in a state of sin, it is impossible for us to please God. It is an absolute, entire and complete impossibility for us to please God as long as we are in the state of nature—as long as we are in ourselves. We are sinners by nature and by practice, and therefore we cannot believe, we cannot come to God, we cannot draw near to him to be accepted by him or to be acceptable to him.

Now when the conviction is brought home to the soul that he is far off from God, that he is a sinner—when he comes to realise under divine teaching (however long that may take or however short the time may take) that he cannot please God—that raises the question in the soul, how is he to draw near to God? How is he to approach God? Scripture reveals and makes known the answer to that question, when-ever it arises in any soul who is conscious of being closed out from God and closed out from God's favour, utterly unable to please God and therefore unable to attain to the favour of God. The Scriptures make known that the Saviour has said, 'I am the way, the truth and the life; no man cometh unto the Father but by me.'

Therefore in order to come to God there must not only be a sense of our sin—because that in itself will not bring us nigh to God—but there must be an understanding, a spiritual understanding, a spiritual enlightenment, with regard to the mediatorial office of the Lord and Saviour Jesus Christ. 'Blessed is the man whom thou dost choose, / and makest approach to thee,' as we were singing in Psalm 65. In the Word of God and in the gospel, a revelation is made of the way in which a sinner may draw near to God. It is through the Lord and Saviour Jesus Christ. He has opened a new and a living way, which he has consecrated through the rent veil of his flesh, by which sinners may draw nigh to God. And when the Holy Spirit makes known to the soul that Christ is the way, then the soul comes to see that Christ is the way because of his atoning work. The new and living way is consecrated through the rent veil of his flesh. During the past days we were engaged in commemorating the rending of the flesh of the Son of God—Christ's body being broken and his blood being shed, when he offered himself as a divine sacrifice to satisfy divine justice. He came to be wounded for our transgressions, and bruised for our iniquities, and pierced for the sins of his people, in order that they might have a way whereby they might draw near to God. They now have a way whereby they may draw near to him, believing that he is, believing he is who he is, believing that he is holy and just, believing that they themselves are sinners, and yet seeing and understanding that Christ is the new and the living way, a way consistent with all the claims of God's nature, a way in which God is waiting to be gracious.

Now, as you can see from Psalm 65, the expression 'coming unto God' embraces the idea of the worship of God. 'Blessed is the man whom thou dost choose / and makest approach to thee.' What next? 'That he within thy courts, O Lord, / may still a dweller be.' The soul is drawn to the courts of God's house and comes to God in this way. Of course that involves the revelation of his Word that God is in Christ, and that he is reconciling sinners to himself. Therefore the soul that comes to God through Christ has a spiritual understanding of the work that Christ did, a spiritual understanding of the person who died and the work that he did, and of the love that was manifested in that work. What love to souls, what love to sinners, was manifested in the death of the Son of God in our nature! He opened up this way so that sinners may draw near to God to enjoy his favour and to enjoy his blessing and to enjoy pardon and peace with him.

This coming to God is also bound up with a drawing by God. 'Blessed is the man whom thou dost choose / and makest approach to thee.' That is just exactly what the Saviour himself said. 'No man cometh unto me, except the Father draw him.' The Father draws the soul by the Holy Spirit. The soul is drawn by the Holy Spirit taking of the things of Christ and revealing them to the soul, making them known to the soul so that he understands and sees how God is glorified in receiving a sinner, and pardoning that sinner's sins for Christ's sake. Through the work of the Holy Spirit the soul sees that this is a way in which God delights. God, who delights in mercy and has no pleasure in the death of him that dieth, has pleasure in this—in souls coming to him, drawing nigh to him through the Lord and Saviour Jesus Christ. So faith has this element in it, this spiritual understanding of God as a just God and a Saviour. Faith has a spiritual understanding of how Christ is the way, and how the death of Christ is the way, and how the love of Christ and the love of the Father is revealed in connection with that, and the Holy Spirit draws the soul effectually.

Believing that God is the rewarder of them that diligently seek him

In faith there is also a belief with regard to God, that 'he is the rewarder of them that diligently seek him'. This raises again the point that when you speak about faith you must speak about the promise of God. Faith without the promise of God has no strength at all, but faith is in the promise, and faith exercises itself on the promise of God.

Faith, you see, includes understanding and being enlightened with regard to the way to God through the divine Redeemer. When the Lord says, 'Seek and ye shall find,' faith believes that, and faith comes to God believing that, believing that those who seek shall find. Faith comes to God as the God who has said, 'I have not said to the seed of Jacob, Seek ye me in vain.' Faith believes that it is not a vain thing to seek the Lord. As we were singing in Psalm 63, David did not think it was a vain thing. He said, 'Lord, thee my God I'll early seek: / my soul doth thirst for thee; / my flesh longs in a dry parched land, / wherein no waters be.'

There is great encouragement in the promises and the exhortations and the invitations which are extended to the soul. God is encouraging souls to seek him, and every encouragement of every description and kind is given for souls to seek the Lord that they may live. Without faith it is impossible to please God. They must believe that he is, and then they must also have this view of him, that he is merciful, that he is to be found, that he is a rewarder of those who diligently seek him. 'Seek and ye shall find.' The reward, of course, is the finding. As you remember, when Dr Duncan met the woman who was selling matches in the streets of Edinburgh, he said to her, 'Now, you be seeking him, and although your seeking will not save you, your finding will.' Although your seeking will not save you, your finding will—in essence that's what we have here.

40

The reward for the seeker is that he will find—that's the promise. In the soul where faith has been wrought and where faith is coming into a living exercise, there is a spiritual understanding and appreciation of this, that God is encouraging sinners to come to him. There is every encouragement in the Word of God for sinners to seek the Lord that they may live—it's full of encouragement for sinners so to do. It is in coming by this new and living way, coming by faith in Christ and being united to Christ, that the soul is accepted in the beloved. They are accepted in the beloved. They are not saved because of their faith. They are not saved because of their seeking. They are saved because of their union to Christ. Their sins are pardoned because of their union to Christ. And that is why preachers of the gospel must be most careful to make this point crystal clear, as Dr Duncan did in that very good phrase, 'Your seeking will not save you, but your finding will.' And once the sinner has found, hopefully he is able to say in the exercise of faith and hope, as was said on another occasion, 'We have found the Messiah.' They are united to Christ. In him, they are pleasing to God. Their sins are forgiven, they are justified by faith, they are saved in the Lord with an everlasting salvation and they are pleasing to him in their persons.

Enoch's service to God

As I was stressing on the last occasion with respect to Abel, he was pleasing to God in his person. In order to have an acceptable service to God, we must be united to Christ, our sins must be forgiven, we must have a warm hearted love for God in Christ, and we must be willing to serve him. That is what was true of Enoch. Enoch was of course a preacher of the Word of God, as we read in the book of Jude. He lived in a very ungodly generation. As we see from Jude, his witness was against the ungodliness around him. He prophesied that the Lord would come to execute judgment upon all, and to convince all that are ungodly among them of their ungodly deeds, and so on. He was living in a particularly evil generation, and because of his faith this is what he testified. He had been brought to know God, and brought to know God in Christ—he was one in whose heart was the law of

God, in whose heart was the principle of holiness. Therefore he testified against the wickedness of the generation in which he lived, just as Noah did later on, discharging his service to God as a preacher of righteousness in his own generation.

As we can see from the record given, Enoch was what we would call 'a law preacher'—that is to say, he was a preacher of the law, he preached the law of God against ungodliness. That did not mean to say that he did not preach the gospel—he did—but he was eminently a preacher of the law of God. Enoch was one who walked with God and lived a life of faith on the God who had brought him to himself and united him to his beloved Son. And as he walked with God, he was conscious of the holiness of God and the righteousness of God, and so sin was to him exceedingly sinful. That is why there sprang from Enoch a testimony against ungodliness, as it did in the case of David when he said, 'Rivers of water run down mine eyes, when I see how men go on in sin, and do not keep thy law.' That is the way in which David's piety and godliness were manifested. There are some who think that all that they should do is preach about the love of Christ. That is a necessary element—but this is very important also, and especially in an ungodly age—that the doctrine of the law of God, the character of God, his holiness and his justice needs to be preached, and a witness needs to be raised against the sins of the generation.

Enoch was not found, because God had translated him

The expression used in connection with Enoch here is that 'he was not found'. Naturally you ask the question, who was trying to find him? Who was looking for him? Who was searching for him? Well, my own opinion in connection with this is that it's the ungodly who were searching for him, that the ungodly had the ire of their carnal mind raised against this preacher of righteousness, this eminently godly man. His witness was of such a nature that he incurred what Christ warned about: 'The world hateth you.' He told his disciples they were to remember that the world hated him before it hated them—that this was what he himself had to endure. Away back there in the Old Testament dispensation, this is what Enoch had to endure as he preached.

42

He had raised the testimony that he had, because he had faith and because he had a walk of faith, because he had communion with God and he walked with God—and the enemy sought him to bring to an end his witness. It will ever be the desire of Satan and the children of Satan to bring to an end a faithful witness. Here I believe they were searching for Enoch but they could not find him, they were not permitted to find him.

God made it plain with regard to Enoch, that Enoch pleased him, that Enoch was a true servant of his. He made it plain in this outstanding and remarkable way, that he translated him. There was Enoch, walking with God, walking by faith—and as he walked by faith and served God by faith, he was translated that he should not see death. God took him, body and soul, into heaven.

When you think of Enoch being translated, your mind goes also to Elijah. Elijah was another preacher of righteousness in an ungodly generation. What a clear witness he raised in the days of Ahab and Jezebel, against the idolatry that existed then! On Mount Carmel he had the testimony that he pleased God. And as you remember, he went away, body and soul, to heaven in the whirlwind. He was taken away. That generation wasn't allowed to lay its hands on him.

But you see, that did not happen to any other eminent preacher of righteousness. You have Enoch translated, and you have Elijah being carried away in the whirlwind, but these are exceptional cases. When you come to John the Baptist, who was the last of the prophets, and who was the greatest of them, because he was the forerunner of the Messiah (and what a wonderful witness he was to the Messiah, by divine grace!)—yet his enemies were allowed to find him. As you remember, he was lying in prison and he was beheaded. He was not translated. Although he came in the power and the spirit of Elias, nevertheless it did not happen in his case.

And that shows you that the Lord is sovereign in his ways of dealing with his servants, and we are not to expect that he will deal in the same way with them all. There they were, Enoch and Elijah and John the Baptist—eminent men of God and faithful servants of

Christ—and two of them were taken away to heaven out of this world, body and soul, translated out of time into eternity, and glorified, as to their bodies and as to their souls—and John the Baptist in the prison had his head removed by his enemies. They found John the Baptist! It did not please the Lord to translate John the Baptist, and yet what praise the Saviour had for him, that among those who were born of women there was not a greater than John the Baptist, this eminent child of God, this eminent prophet and eminent witness! As to his soul he went to heaven as surely as Enoch and Elijah's souls and bodies did, and he will yet go as to his body too—the body that was beheaded for Jesus's sake. He will be raised on the morning of the resurrection, and his body will be made like unto the glorious body of the divine Redeemer. Therefore we see how God deals, not only with his servants but with all his people, in a way that is most for his glory and most for their good eventually.

And therefore let us seek grace that we would be of them and that we would have the faith that is mentioned here, without which it is impossible to please God. If we are destitute of this faith we cannot be united to Christ. There is no merit in faith itself; it is after all the gift of God. But by virtue of union to Christ believers are accepted in the beloved.

And let us seek to lay hold on this great fact, that we are encouraged to seek the Lord. He has never said to the seed of Jacob, 'Seek ye me in vain.' There is great encouragement to seek the Lord while he may be found, and to call upon him while he is near. May the communion season and the means of grace in the Word give us to see and to understand this, that the Lord is waiting to be gracious and that he is encouraging us to seek him. However great our sins may be, however multitudinous they may be, however vile they may be, we are invited to draw near to him, to taste and see that God is good.

May he bless his Word.

4 Seeking and finding God

HEBREWS 11:6

But without faith it is impossible to please him: for he that cometh to God must believe that he is, and that he is a rewarder of them that diligently seek him.

LORD'S DAY EVENING, 28TH FEBRUARY 1999

IN this part of the Word of God the apostle speaks a great deal about faith. At the beginning of the chapter we are given the only definition we have of faith in the Word of God. We are told that faith is the gift of God, and we know it to be a grace of the Holy Ghost, but we don't have anywhere else an explanation of what faith is except here at the beginning of this chapter. 'Now faith is the substance of things hoped for, the evidence of things not seen.'

We are also told in this chapter that by faith the elders obtained a good report. The elders are the ancients, the ones in the Old Testament dispensation—Abraham and Isaac and Jacob and all those who were born in the time of the church's childhood, before it came to maturity in the days in which you and I live, that is, the last days, the New Testament times. By faith, the elders obtained a good report. They pleased God. That was above everything else. As we read with regard to Enoch, 'by faith he was translated that he should not see death,' and 'before his translation he had this testimony'—that is the good report—'that he pleased God'. There was a good testimony with regard to Abraham, with regard to Isaac, with regard to Jacob, with regard to Noah, with regard to Enoch. They lived by faith in this

45

world. Out of the whole human family, they were the ones who were well pleasing to God. Out of the multitudes and multitudes of the human race, these were the ones who obtained a good report, a good testimony with regard to themselves. For example, those of this faith declared plainly that they sought a country, and it was a country that was not seen—it was a country that could not been seen with the eyes of the body. But faith, as we read in the definition here, is the substance of things hoped for, the evidence of things not seen. Where faith is, a conviction is wrought in the heart about things that cannot be seen with the bodily eye, but they can be seen with the eye of faith, and they are real to the eye of faith—so real that the conduct of the person in whom faith is, is governed by the view they have by faith.

Let us just pause for a moment to speak about natural faith. For instance, I have never been in the city of Wellington in New Zealand. But I know many people who have been there, and who have told me about 'Windy Wellington', and I believe there is such a place although I have never seen it. I have not seen it with my eyes, but I have evidence that it is there. Although I've never seen Wellington yet I believe it is there because I have the evidence of things not seen. Now, that is a natural faith. But this faith here is faith which is spiritual—it is to do with things that are not seen, in the sense that they are spiritual. I recently heard an atheist speak on the radio, and he said that he had not met anybody who had seen God. Just imagine the sheer ignorance of such a man! God is a spirit, and you cannot see a spirit with the eyes of the body. But a far greater man than this atheist was Moses, and Moses 'endured, as seeing him who is invisible'. Why? Because Moses had faith. And this atheist had no faith—or no spiritual faith, I should say—therefore he made these ridiculous remarks as though he was very wise and as though that was an end of all argument. But we know better than atheists. The Word of God teaches us better, that 'faith is the evidence of things not seen'.

That's why the elders were travelling to a better country, a heavenly country, a country that could not been seen, a country on the other side of death—a country where Christ is, whom they never saw with the eyes of the body. Abraham saw Christ's day by the eye of faith in the promise given to him, that 'in thy seed shall all the nations of the earth be blessed'. He never saw Christ with his bodily eyes, but he was journeying Zion-ward, he was journeying to that place where Christ is now. As to his soul, he is there with Christ now, although his body lies now in Hebron under the mosque that has been built there by Muslims. You see, heaven was real to Abraham. It was an evidence he had in faith, an evidence of things not seen. It was real, so that he was journeying to this country. He could have returned back to another country, but he did not do so—he desired 'a better country, that is, an heavenly: wherefore God is not ashamed to be called their God: for he hath prepared for them a city', a city on the other side of death. The elders were journeying to that city. And so are God's people in this day and generation of ours. They are doing so because they have faith, because they believe that Christ is there, and because they believe that there are the other people who have died in Christ, those who are described in the Word of God in these words, 'blessed are the dead that die in the Lord'—they are united to Christ and they rest from their labours, and their works do follow them. So faith is a great possession. It is a great possession, and it is absolutely necessary.

'He cometh unto God must believe that he is, and that he is a rewarder of them that diligently seek him.' 'Whatsoever is not of faith is sin' (Romans 14:23). Without the grace of faith, it is impossible to please God, no matter what may be pleasing to the outward eye and pleasing and apparently in the form of godliness. 'For he that cometh unto God must believe that he is.' Of course faith believes the whole of the Word of God from Genesis to Revelation, but it begins here, that 'he must believe that he is'—that he exists, that there is such a divine being as God.

Now this Sabbath evening we are here and we are embraced by the words, 'he that cometh unto God'. He that comes to the worship of God, that comes to engage in the worship of God, he must believe that God is. Now is that true of you? This Sabbath evening when you came to the house of God, did you come to this house of prayer with a desire, with an expectation that God would meet with you? Or did you just come because you have been in the habit of coming and because you would feel out of place if you didn't come, and you want to hear a minister preach? But you see the key to the thing is this, that he that cometh unto God must believe that he is.

1. Therefore we shall begin by considering this great matter. In the soul of those who come to God there must be an understanding and an apprehension and a sense of the divine being.

2. Then the second thing that we shall consider is that in the soul that comes to God there must be a realisation of the fact that he can be found. We sang in the psalm of God saying, 'Seek ye my face' (Psalm 27:8). And he never said—never—never this Sabbath evening, surely, as every other Sabbath day, as in every other generation from ancient times—he never said to the seed of Jacob, 'seek ye me in vain' (Isaiah 45:19). 'When thou didst say, Seek ye my face, then thus did my heart reply, Thy face, Lord, seek will I.' There you have a realisation that God is to be found.

3. Finally, God is to be found in the sense that he is the rewarder of all those who diligently seek him. The reward is to find him. It is not a reward reckoned of debt, it is not a reward reckoned because of merits of ours or even the merit of seeking, but there is a reward in finding him.

1. He that cometh to God must believe that he is
Now in order to explain this more fully, we shall consider what happened to Abraham, who is spoken of in this chapter under his later name of Abraham. You may remember when the five kings went away with his nephew Lot, Abraham took those who were trained in his own house, went after the kings, and defeated them in the battle. When one of the kings wanted to give Abraham a reward he refused it, because he wouldn't allow a heathen king to be able to say, 'I made Abraham rich' (Genesis 14:8–24). But then Abraham must have felt he was alone in the land among these Canaanitish tribes—he must have been afraid that these kings would realign and come to attack

him again. Therefore God came to him and said, 'Fear not, Abram' (Genesis 15:1), and he made an oath about these kings.

You see, when God says, 'Fear not,' he gives an explanation of why you shouldn't fear. Do you know anything about that? Do you know anything about God saying to your soul, 'Fear not,' then giving an explanation of why you should not fear? He opens your understanding to see why you should not fear. What the Lord said to godly Abraham was, 'Fear not, for I am thy shield, and thy exceeding great reward.' That is why there is no reason to fear. You don't need a heathen shield and buckler, you don't need all these young men who were defending your house—you don't need them, because I am thy shield. And I am 'thy exceeding great reward'. Abraham refused to be made rich by the heathen, because the Lord was his reward.

And there is Moses, to illustrate this point again. Moses was brought up in the palace as the son of Pharaoh's daughter, and the whole of the Egyptian empire, the greatest empire of that time in history, stretched out before him—it was all his. It was all his, but Moses refused, just like Abraham. The Lord's people are not to be influenced by bribes from pagans. It would be a good thing if our rulers would learn that lesson when they are being pushed around by the nations in Europe that we defeated in the war. The people of God are not like that—they're not going to be indebted to the world. Abraham wasn't, and nor was Moses. All this was lying before him— to be the emperor, to have the riches, the pleasures of sin, the security—the glory of the kingdom of Egypt would all be his. And he refused it. He refused it by faith, and he chose to suffer affliction with the people of God rather than have a whole kingdom, and a whole empire. He chose to be with the people of God, the suffering people of God, those who were to travel through the wilderness, because he had respect unto the recompense of the reward. The reward was that the God of Israel would be his God, the cup of his inheritance and his portion for ever and ever. He chose that. Why? Because he had the grace of faith, that's why. You see how important it is, and how we need to be considering this matter very, very carefully—each one for himself and for herself—that without faith it is impossible to please God, for he that cometh to God must believe that he is.

Now there are two ways in which God reveals himself. One is in his works, and the other is in his Word. Here are the children of men, considering the works of God in creation. Let us take a small example to illustrate this particular point. You think of the human body. You think of the eye framed for seeing, the ear framed for hearing—think of all the members of the body. Each one has its own place, and each one operates according to the impress of a creative power. The body is a wonderful thing. Now you get people in the world of medicine, and they speak about the wonders of the body. But they do not see God. They are faced with the fact that the human body is beyond the power of man to form, in all its intricacies, in all its systems. Although they see the wonder of the body and they speak about the wonder of nature, yet they do not see God. They'll tell some of their patients when they restore their limbs, 'We cannot do it as nature did it.' They don't say, 'We cannot do it as God did it'—because they do not see God in it.

Then again, you take the creation of the world. You take people viewing the scenery of the world—the poetry that is written, the songs that are made with regard to the beauties of creation—but they do not see God. They see the beauties of creation, and enjoy it, because it appeals to their senses, but they do not see God in it.

They do not see God in his works. Why is that? Because the fool says in his heart, 'There is no God.' That is of course the wish of his heart. That atheist who was speaking on the radio said he had never met anybody who had seen God, and he had never seen him, and he would like to think because of that, that there is no God, that God doesn't exist. He would like to think that—that the God who created the world does not exist. But this is the God of infinite power, before whom the nations of the world are like the small dust in the balance, which the merchant doesn't bother to sweep away when he weighs out the goods, it is so insignificant. So the whole human race and the empires of the world are in the sight of the creator of the ends of the earth. He is a God of infinite power and glory and majesty, and a God who has said that sin is 'that abominable thing which I hate'. But, as we are told, men are in possession of the carnal mind which is enmity—enmity against God—and they are without God and without hope in the world. Men as they are by nature are of that kind. Therefore there is this hatred to God. Therefore they will not accept that God is creator. That's what's behind it. It's the carnal mind—graceless, godless men under the influence of the carnal mind.

But as we see, God has also revealed himself in the Scriptures of the Old and New Testaments. The revelation there in the Word is more glorious, more wonderful, than the revelation in the works of God. There shines in the firmament of the Word of God, not the natural sun which shines in the firmament of the created universe, which traverses its course in the created heavens, but the sun of right-eousness—the Son of God in your nature and mine. And the glory of God shines in every page of Holy Writ, as the sun of righteousness, which rises progressively from Genesis to Revelation. This revelation is more glorious than the revelation of God's glory that the heavens declare or his handworks which the skies preach. And yet the heart of man is filled with enmity—with enmity!—against the Word of God! With greater enmity than against God as creator. Why? Because the natural man has no faith. And these atheists and pagans, they forget that there are people in this world who have faith. And faith is the gift of God, wrought in the hearts by the Holy Ghost.

Now, 'he that cometh unto God must believe that he is'. The Holy Spirit brings home to this soul here and that soul there that God is. Some of you here, sitting in the pews in this congregation this Sabbath evening, you know this. There was a time when God was not in all your thoughts. You didn't think about him. You just spent your days in vanity and lies, without any thought of God. But then a time came when this took possession of your soul, that God is.

'He that cometh unto God must believe that he is,' and therefore when the Holy Spirit is working faith in the soul he begins here—by giving a sense to the soul of the being of God, that God is. He gives that sense first of all with regard to God as creator. As we are told here, 'Through faith we understand that the worlds were framed by the word of God.' It is God's testimony that he is the creator of the ends of the earth, who neither faints nor is weary. The soul who has come to believe that God is—that the great God of eternity exists after all, and that he is the creator of the ends of the earth—that soul starts to realise, 'I am a creature of God, and therefore I am responsible to God. God created me and therefore I am responsible to God for my conduct in his eyes, and all things are naked and opened unto the eyes of him with whom we have to do.' Believing that God is, the soul realises that God is the creator of the ends of the earth, that he is the lawgiver, that he is the ultimate judge. And when this is brought into the soul by the Spirit of God, convincing the soul that the Word that we have from Genesis to Revelation is the Word of that God—the soul comes to have what we might call an apprehension of the being of God, a sense that God is.

And bound up with that sense in the soul that God is, is a realisation that I am far from God. Now if you are here and the Holy Spirit has awakened your soul, that's what you have discovered—not only that God was, not only that he was holy, just and unchangeable, not only that he was the creator of the ends of his earth and that you were his creature—but that you were at a distance from God. To 'come to God' implies that there is a distance from God, a distance between your soul and God. 'He that cometh unto God' is far from God—a prodigal son or a prodigal daughter in the far country, separated by their sins from God, dwelling without God and without hope in the world, living for the world and the ways of the world, to satisfy the lust of the flesh and the lust of the eyes and the pride of life. But he that cometh unto God must believe that he is, and believe that he has lost God's favour—that he is under God's displeasure on account of his sin, that he is at a great distance from God, a distance that he can never cover or overcome by himself.

We read in one place in the Song of Solomon about mountains which are called the 'mountains of Bether'. And the Hebrew word 'bether' means division—they are the mountains of division. Now the soul that comes to believe that God is, is a soul that comes to believe there are mountains of division between his soul and God, and these mountains are the mountains of the guilt of his sins—the mountains of his sins between his soul and God. And the conviction is wrought in his heart that he can never traverse these mountains. He cannot come to God as long as these mountains are there. The journey is too great for him.

Yet, at the same time, the same Holy Spirit who is teaching the soul and who is working faith in the soul puts a desire in that soul to seek God—to seek the God whose favour they have lost, to seek the God from whom they are separated, to seek the God who is revealed in the Word of God as the God who is holy and just in all his ways. That desire is put in the soul.

And there are some of God's people—we do not say all, for the Holy Spirit is sovereign in his working—who remember that sense of desire far more vividly than any terrifying sense they had of God's displeasure. For instance, if you read about the conversion of a man like M'Cheyne, he did not have any particular alarming sense of God's displeasure, but a calm, continuous realisation that he was a sinner before God. John Bunyan of course was different, and others were different again. The apostle Paul says himself, 'Knowing the terror of the Lord, we persuade men.' But the Holy Spirit is sovereign. There are some of God's people, and although they felt the divine displeasure, and they felt that God was angry with the wicked every day, nevertheless what was predominant in their experience was that this desire was put into their souls, to seek God.

2. The coming soul realises that God is to be found

So we see here that faith embraces not only the conviction that God is, and that he is the creator, but it embraces also the view that God is to be found. There is put in the soul a realisation that the God whom they lost, the God whose favour they lost, is a God who is now to be found.

Indeed, he is encouraging souls to seek his face. He is saying, 'Seek ye my face!' 'Though your sins be as scarlet, they shall be as white as snow; though they be red like crimson, they shall be as wool.' 'Ever seek my face, seek me because I am to be found!' And where is he to be found? He is to be found in the place where the Word of God says, 'God was in Christ, reconciling the world to himself.' That is where he is to be found. He is to be found in Christ. And he holds himself forth as one who is to be found when he says, 'Seek ye my face, seek me as I am to be found in Christ, as the God of peace who brought again from the dead the Lord Jesus, that great Shepherd of the sheep.' He is to be found in Christ.

God was in Christ reconciling the world unto himself. And who is this person, Christ? Well, you have heard about him again and again. Are you becoming acquainted with him? Do you know him? Does he speak to you? Do you speak to him? Do you praise him? Do you love him? Do you embrace him when you hear about him in the Word of God, that he is the Son of the Father in truth and love? He is the one who said, 'No man hath seen God at any time; the only begotten Son, which is in the bosom of the Father, he hath declared him.' He has revealed him in this way—not only as the Son of his love but as the Saviour of the lost, and the undone, and the ruined and the hell-deserving. God was in Christ, providing in Christ a Saviour for the chief of sinners. Christ is the one who came in the fulness of the times into this world, the one in whom the promise given to Abraham was fulfilled, that 'in thee and thy seed shall all the nations of the earth be blessed'. That seed was not Isaac, but that seed was the Isaac of the New Testament, that seed was Christ. In Christ all the nations of the earth were to be blessed. It is in Christ that God is to be found as the God of peace.

And God is found as the God of peace in connection with the work that the Saviour carried out when he came into the world. We are told in the Word of God that when the fulness of the times came, Christ came into the world. And the way in which he came into the world was that he was born of a woman. Now you know that Christ as the Son of God has all the attributes of deity, and therefore in his person he is omnipresent. And the omnipresence of God means that the whole of the divine being is at every point of space at every moment of time. Now that is a great concept—the omnipresence of God—that the whole, not a part, but the whole of the divine nature is at every point of space at every moment of time. As the psalmist said, 'Ascend I heaven, lo, thou art there; / there if in hell I lie' (Psalm 139:8). But that is a different thing from Christ's coming into the world, when he took finite human nature into union with his divine person. See, you must understand that. The Son of God has the attribute of omnipresence because he has the possession of the divine nature. But his coming into the world was a different thing altogether. Great is the mystery of godliness.

Two mysteries in particular are mentioned in the Scripture (and remember that a mystery is something that would not be known unless it was revealed). One is the mystery of godliness, and the mystery of godliness is Christ. The mystery of godliness—the Son of God in your nature and mine—the Son of God in the fulness of his divine person, with a holy humanity united to that divine nature. Great is the wonder of how the Son of God, the Son of the Father in truth and love, came into this world, born of a woman. This is the mystery of godliness. But we are told also that there is another mystery, and that is the mystery of iniquity. The mystery of iniquity is the antichrist, the pope of Rome. That is revealed in the Word of God just as surely as the mystery of godliness. As the mystery of godliness is Christ, so the mystery of iniquity is the papal system. And how much the people of this country need to learn that, as well as the religious leaders! But they don't know the mystery of godliness. They have no experimental knowledge of Christ. Some of these religious leaders have no more knowledge of the Saviour than the most unenlightened heathen. It's clear they don't understand the mystery of godliness, and therefore they do not understand the mystery of iniquity.

But this is the mystery of godliness, the Son of God being born of a woman. He who was and is the eternal Son of the Father, to whom belongs the throne of eternity, above every law and above his own law, was born of a woman, made under the law. Under the law! Do you think of that? Do you think of the Son of God, the brightness of the Father's glory, the express image of his person, coming under his own holy law, the law that he has given to you and to me, the law that we have broken? He comes under that law, to render obedience to that law, in the room and place of his people, of whom we read that they are the seed of Abraham, like the stars of the sky for multitude, and the grains of sand by the sea shore in number.

The Son of God came! He came in your nature and mine. And the day that he came out of the womb of Mary, he was made under the law, to render obedience to the law in the room and the place of that multitude. The law of God required an obedience that would satisfy it with regard to this multitude. And this person was to render that obedience. How could that be? How could the man Christ Jesus render obedience to the holy, spiritual, good law of God in the room of such a number? Only because he was not a mere man—because of the mystery of godliness. It was the Son of God who was made under the law in your nature and mine. It was the Son of God in your nature and mine who rendered obedience to the law of God. Therefore that obedience was of infinite value, of eternal value, of unchangeable value—it was an obedience that rendered complete satisfaction to the law of God on behalf of this innumerable multitude.

But more than that was needed. Not just that he would be obedient from the womb of Mary down through the thirty years he was in this world, but that he would also be obedient unto death. And not just a natural death, but the death of the cross, the death of dying under the curse of God's law poured out on him as he stood in the room and place of the guilty who deserved eternal death. That curse was emptied on him. Christ has redeemed us from the curse of the law, being made a curse for us. The curse of God became his death on the cross of Calvary, and it became his death until the curse was emptied of that death, and he cried on the cross, 'It is finished!' 'The curse is over and done with, the curse is empty, the curse is done, and my people are redeemed!'—not with corruptible things such as silver and gold, but with the precious blood of Christ, as of a lamb without spot and without blemish. 'So now,' says God, 'seek ye my face! Seek me where I am to be found—in Christ!'

Yes, God was in Christ, reconciling the world unto himself. He is there reconciling sinners to himself—he is to be found there as the God of peace, the God of infinite love, as the God who is rich in mercy—he is to be found in Christ. Therefore he says, 'Seek ye my face!' He says to your soul and to mine, 'Seek me as the God who is in Christ, reconciling the world unto himself, the God of peace!'

3. God is a rewarder of those who diligently seek him

So this is wrought in the heart in connection with the grace of faith: the soul comes to see that this God can be found by a guilty sinner, and that the way in which he can come near to God is through Christ. Through God in Christ he can be reconciled. Through God in Christ the mountains of Bether can be taken away. His soul can flee into the bosom of God in Jesus Christ. 'I am thy shield and thy exceeding great reward' is what God said to Abraham. God was the cup of his inheritance, as David said. God himself is his reward.

This is the reward, and it is a reward bound up with seeking him and finding him. It is a reward not reckoned of debt, any more than it was in the case of Moses. You remember what we were reading with regard to Moses. When he chose to suffer affliction with the people of God, rather than to enjoy the pleasures of sin for a season, it was because he had respect to the recompense of the reward. The recompense of the reward was that God would be his God for ever and ever, and would guide him even unto death. That is what is meant here. He is a rewarder of the soul that finds him. To anyone who has found what Abraham found, God says to him, 'I am not only thy shield but I am also thy exceeding great reward.' To have God as your possession—to have the God against whom you sinned to be the cup of your inheritance—will make you able to say with David, 'Surely unto me the lines in pleasant places fell; / yea the inheritance I got / in beauty doth excel!' (Psalm 16:6). What is your inheritance, David?

It is to have God in Christ as my portion for ever and ever, and to be reconciled to him and to have an entrance into his love and his favour, to be enjoying communion and fellowship with the Father and with the Son.

Now your seeking of him, of course, is to be according to the rule of the Word of God. Therefore God has set up means of grace in the world—means wherein he reveals himself and Christ reveals himself. You remember, in the Song of Solomon, that the beloved stood by the wall, then he showed himself through the lattice. When he was standing by the wall there was separation, a barrier between them. But then he showed himself through the lattice to his beloved, to his people. These lattices are the means of grace—the Word of God read, the Word of God preached, the throne of grace where we have the right to come with boldness that we may obtain mercy and grace to help in time of need. All the means of grace in the world are set up by God in order that he might say to the soul, 'Seek ye my face!' When you are here this Sabbath evening, whoever you are, you have these means of grace—the reading of the Word of God, the singing of the praises of God, the prayer to God—and in all of these, God is saying to you—yes, to you!—not to the man beside you, not to the woman behind you, but to you!—he is saying, 'Seek ye my face!' What will your heart say now? Do you know that God is? Do you know that you need salvation? Do you know that you need to be reconciled to God? Is your heart saying, 'Thy face, Lord, I will seek'? 'Thus did my heart reply, Thy face, Lord, seek will I.' Is that true of you this Sabbath evening?

The means of grace are there for the diligent seeking, for the earnest seeking, the longing seeking. As we read in Psalm 63, 'Lord, thee my God I'll early seek; / my soul doth thirst for thee; / my flesh longs in a dry parched land, / wherein no waters be.' Is this world a dry, parched land to you? Remember the old man in Argyll who Neil Cameron wrote about. Mr Cameron tells about this old man, that when he was on his deathbed he asked to be carried outside so that he would have a last view of the hills and the dales of his native land.

They took him out and he looked round and he said, 'It is a bonny world, but what made it a bonny world to me was that I found Christ here.' Now, is that true of you? For without faith it is impossible to please God, for he that cometh to God must believe that he is, and that he is a rewarder of them that diligently seek him, and those that seek shall find.

May he bless his Word.

5 Coming to God

HEBREWS 11:6

But without faith it is impossible to please him: for he that cometh to God must believe that he is, and that he is a rewarder of them that diligently seek him

WEDNESDAY, 11TH JANUARY 2006

T HESE are very solemn words. You remember the disciples asking the Saviour the question, 'Who then can be saved?' And the Saviour replied, 'With men it is impossible; but with God all things are possible.' Now here is God saying that there is something that is impossible. That is, in drawing nigh to God it is impossible to please him apart from faith. That is what he says here. That is why these words are so solemn. The Saviour said, 'With God all things are possible,' and here is God himself saying in his Word that something is impossible. It is impossible to please God if we approach him without faith. We read of Enoch that before he was translated he had this testimony, that he pleased God. And it is in the light of that that we read these solemn words. They are of course applicable to our occasions of drawing near to God. We draw near to God in public worship, when we must have faith in living exercise—we draw near to God in family worship, when we must have faith in living exercise—and we must have faith when we draw near to God privately, as individuals, when there is no one there but ourselves. We must have this faith in exercise if our drawing near is to be pleasing to God.

Now on this occasion I wish to confine myself to the first time that a sinner comes to God; that is, at the time of the conversion of that soul. That is the time when faith comes into exercise in a living way. Faith is wrought in the heart of a sinner by the Spirit of God in effectual calling. And these words set before us in a very clear way what faith is—this faith, the faith without which it is impossible to please God. Now people may read about faith and they hear people saying that faith includes knowledge, assent and trust. This is one way of describing faith. But here we have faith described for us by way of example. The way in which faith is exercised is brought before us here in a very clear and solemn way, and that is what we shall endeavour to consider at the present time.

Believing that God is

The first thing with regard to faith which we are told here by the Holy Spirit through the apostle Paul writing to the Hebrews, is that 'he that cometh to God must believe that he is'. That is the first matter in connection with faith being wrought in the heart. If you were to be asked the question, 'Do you believe in God?' you would all say, 'Oh yes, of course. We go to church, we read the Bible, we go to the prayer meeting.' But this is something else. This is a belief that *God is*. The Holy Spirit gives a sense to the soul that *God is*. Before then, the sinner is not conscious of God, or of his presence, except in a nominal way. But now he has a sense in his soul that God is. And I do not mean by that merely a sense of the being of God, but also that the Holy Spirit gives to the soul a sense that God is a glorious being, holy, just and unchangeable, a God of infinite majesty and glory, and that he is our God. The soul feels that in his conscience, in the faculties of his soul. 'There is this being, this glorious being, and I now know that he is, because it has been brought into my soul by this gracious power, and he is my God, and I am responsible to him.'

Now we have a good illustration of it in the reference made to Abraham. He was then named Abram and was in Ur of the Chaldees. He was a pagan, he was full of the idolatry that filled the world at that time, and many think—and I agree—because of his name—that he was actually a priest in that idolatrous situation. What happened? 'The God of glory appeared to our father Abraham,' Stephen said. That's what I'm talking about—in the midst of all this darkness, the Holy Spirit imparted to Abraham's soul a sense of the being of God. He believed that God was a glorious being—a God of holiness, of justice, the God of power—and he believed that in his soul. That was the first step to him then feeling the weight of that glory behind the command given to him by God. And that shows you that he felt in his soul that this was his God.

The distance between the sinner and God

Now the second thing that's brought before us here is that the soul is represented as coming to God. That implies that there is a great distance between this God and the soul.

What the Holy Spirit does is to give to the soul a sense of the fact that he or she is far from God. Your sins and your iniquities have separated between you and your God. So the soul is made conscious in his own heart, or in his own experience, of this great distance. He is like the prodigal son in the far country, far away. Although up to that moment he is engaged in satisfying the lusts of the flesh and the lust of the eyes and the pride of life, he now comes to realise the greatness of the distance between himself and God—he therefore realises that he is in a state of condemnation and a state in which he is ready to perish. He is ready to perish before this God of holiness, the God of purity, the God of justice, and the God who is angry with the sinner every day. As it says, 'The sins of Judah have kindled a fire in mine anger, which shall burn for ever' (Jeremiah 17:4 with verse 1). The Holy Spirit imparts to the soul the sense of how great the distance is between his soul and God.

God is a rewarder of them that diligently seek him

Now here is surely a very remarkable thing with regard to faith. The soul believes, first of all, that God is a glorious being, a God of infinite majesty and power. He believes that God is. And he also believes that he is at a distance from God, to such an extent that he is ready to perish. And yet, we are told here, we must believe that God is 'a rewarder of them that diligently seek him'.

You see the wonder of that! This soul that is ready to perish, the soul that is realising more and more the glory of God and the perfections of God, and therefore his own sinfulness and condemnation—here is the view that the Holy Spirit is now giving him: that this God is a rewarder of them that diligently seek him. This very God that he believes in, and whose glory and power he understands, in a measure—he is a rewarder of them that diligently seek him.

How are we to explain that? Well, we can explain it, of course, if we have experience of it, but let us explain it first of all by enquiring as to this phrase, 'he is a rewarder'—God, this great God, is a rewarder of them that diligently seek him. Most people say, 'That is a reward that is not reckoned of merit, but it is of grace.' Well, I'm not satisfied with that. I don't believe that is the proper explanation. The proper explanation is that when they are brought to diligently seek this God, the reward is that they find him. That's the reward! See what God said to Abraham, 'I am thy shield.' And what else? 'And thy exceeding great reward.' What does David say? 'God is of mine inheritance / and cup the portion.' What does Paul say? 'That I may win Christ.' So the reward mentioned here is when the seeking soul finds God and peace with God.

One of the great examples that sheds remarkable light on this is the case of the prodigal son. There he is, just as in the case of the sinner that I have described already—at great distance from his father's house, ready to perish in the land that is far off; and when he is ready to perish in the far country, something enters his mind—something is imparted to his mind. As he himself says, 'There is food and enough to spare in my father's house, and I perish with hunger!' What now? 'I will arise and go to my father.' There you are! There is the soul now coming to God, and that because he has seen God as a rewarder. He has seen, in the case of the prodigal, bread and enough to spare—but in the case of the sinner, he sees God in Christ, as the Holy Spirit enlightens his mind in the knowledge of Christ, and in the knowledge of the glory of God in Christ. As you remember, the Word of God says, 'God, who commanded the light to shine out of darkness, hath shined in our hearts, to give the light of the knowledge of the glory of God in the face of Jesus Christ.'

Knowledge of the person and work of Christ

Now, what we are to understand by 'the face of Jesus Christ' is first of all the person of Christ. The glory of God shines in the person of Christ—the divine Son of the everlasting Father coming to be united to a human nature and dwelling in that human nature as the appointed and anointed Mediator between God and man—the Saviour who came in God's great name to save. The soul is enlightened in this aspect of the knowledge of God's glory in Christ.

What does he see in Christ's person? Well, he sees many things. But just now he sees two things: one, the divine nature in the person of the Son; two, the human nature, conceived by the power of the Holy Ghost in the womb of a virgin, and united to the divine nature, and the human nature and the divine nature united together, revealing the glory of God in the purpose of salvation, that sinners would be united to him and reconciled to him through the person of Christ.

Then the second thing we are to understand by 'the face of Jesus Christ' is a knowledge of the work of Christ. That work is to do with this great distance between God and the sinner, on account of the sins of the sinner. The Saviour is the Mediator, as I said, or, as I might say, the Lamb of God—he is the Lamb of God, the Lamb of the Father's providing. The sinner gets light on the Word of God and through the Word of God regarding the imputation to the Saviour of the sins of all those who are loved with an everlasting love in the covenant that is ordered in all things and sure. And the sinner gets light regarding Christ's dying for the ungodly. 'When we were yet without strength, in due time Christ died for the ungodly.'

It is there that the sinner begins to see that God is a rewarder of those who diligently seek him. There is every encouragement given in the gospel for sinners to seek to be reconciled to God, and to come into possession of God as their eternal portion. That is what happened in the case of the prodigal son. 'I will arise and go to my father'—that was the beginning of it—diligent seeking. Oh how diligent he was now, seeking to return to his father! And as he was coming home, we have light shed on a matter of great importance in connection with faith. For one thing, he was believing that there was food enough and to spare in his father's house. But there was something else too, and that is, he was confessing. 'I have sinned against heaven and before thee, and am no more worthy to be called thy son; make me as one of thy hired servants.' One of the hired servants was, as it were, just in the back door—he just wanted the lowest place in his father's house. But notice the importance of this: faith and repentance.

It is very necessary for us to understand quite clearly that there is no such thing as faith without repentance. And there is no such thing as repentance without faith. Some theologians say that faith comes into the soul and then it is followed by repentance. Well, the greatest preacher that ever stood on the face of the earth was the Lord Jesus Christ, and when he preached the gospel of the kingdom, he preached, 'Repent and believe the gospel!' It is true that it is faith that receives the mercy of God in Christ—that is true. But faith and repentance are really twin graces. I think it is very important for us to remember that when we are drawing nigh to God—there must be not only faith in the fact that there is salvation enough and to spare in Christ and in God in Christ, but also we must repent of our sins. Sin must be made an evil and a bitter thing to us, so that we truly repent of it, so that we turn from it with grief and hatred.

Many people have terrors of conscience through the common operations of the Holy Spirit. Take the case of Felix. Paul was preaching and Felix trembled. His conscience trembled at his sins when he was hearing Paul preach, but it didn't come to anything. It was like the early cloud and the morning dew. It disappeared. And so it was with Agrippa too, for he felt Paul's preaching of Christ drawing him to Christ. 'Almost', he said, 'thou persuadest me to be a Christian'— but it did not happen. In neither case did they have the repentance which the Holy Spirit works in the soul when he gives saving faith.

They did not come to this—what I'm speaking about here—this faith. The sinner is now, in the phrase used here, diligently seeking.

Seeking and finding the reward

Many of you will remember the well-known phrase of Rabbi Duncan to the old woman. 'You'll be seeking Christ,' he said, 'and although your seeking will not save you, your finding will.' That's what's here—the reward is the finding.

Now the finding that is referred to here, as I believe to be the true sense of the word 'reward', is Christ. The sinner has his seeking times and discouragements and all the rest of it, but he does come to a time when he finds. 'Your finding will save you,' Rabbi Duncan said. That's good theology and it's good scriptural teaching, good experimental teaching, that 'your finding will save you'. It is a finding of Christ, and of God in Christ.

In this finding, light is given to the soul from the Word of God. We read with regard to the two on the way to Emmaus that they said, 'Did not our hearts burn within us while he talked with us by the way and opened to us the Scriptures?' That is the meaning of the words, 'The entrance of thy words giveth light.' It doesn't mean the light of the word entering the soul, but the Scripture being opened so that the soul gets light through the opening of the Scripture. In the finding there is an opening of the Scripture, in which the soul experiences a drawing to Christ. That drawing to Christ is how he finds him. In the light of the Word of God—whether it be one portion, whether it be a sermon, whatever way it may be—it is the opening of the Word of God, and in the light of that Word, the sinner sees Christ and him crucified.

The gospel teaches two aspects of the drawing. The Saviour says, 'If I be lifted up, I will draw all men unto me.' The view that is given to the soul is a view of Christ and him crucified, and a view of his love in giving himself to die for the ungodly, for those who had no help of man at all. The soul is drawn by that, on the one hand. The second form of drawing is also very important. 'No man,' said Christ, 'can come unto me, except the Father draw him.' In this coming to

Christ and in finding Christ by faith, there is an understanding not only of the love of Christ in dying in the room and place of the guilty, but also the love of the Father in giving his Son. The love of the Father!—this God, this great God that the soul came to have an experimental knowledge of! The soul is now brought to see and to wonder at this, that 'herein is love, not that we loved God, but that he loved us, and sent his Son to be the propitiation for our sins.' This is the drawing to Christ that I am speaking about, in which the soul comes to God, and comes to have God in Christ as his possession— finding him, finding Christ, and finding reconciliation to the Father in Christ.

Without faith it is impossible to please him
'Without faith, it is impossible to please God.' Whatever else people may have, whatever else people may think they have, when they draw nigh to God without this faith, it is impossible to please him. For he that cometh to God must believe that he is, and that he is a rewarder of them that diligently seek him.

This is very important in the day in which we live, when very superficial views are given of faith. One would almost think at times, the way that reference is made to this precious gift of God, that faith was something that people kind of 'caught', like catching measles or scarlet fever. They can't give an explanation. How did it happen? How was the grace of faith wrought in your soul? Do you know anything about being convinced that God is? Do you know anything about the distance between your soul and God? Do you know anything about coming near to this glorious person and being reconciled to him, and thus having God as your portion and possession and inheritance for ever and ever? As God said to Abraham, so he says to every soul that comes by faith of the operation of God, standing in the power of God and not in the wisdom of men, 'I am thy exceeding great reward.' He is a rewarder of them that diligently seek him, and that is the reward— to find him. And finding is absolutely necessary. It cannot be stressed too much. Otherwise you fail and come short of the grace of God. The grace that's wrought by the Holy Spirit will never find rest until it finds rest in Christ, the great object of faith, and until it finds rest in the reconciliation that is bound up with faith. Let us remember what we are told here clearly and unmistakeably, that without faith it is impossible to please God. What solemn words! Whatever religion people may have and whatever religious talk and so called religious experiences they have, here is the core of the matter—without faith it is impossible to please him.

Now just one last point and then I'll conclude. Faith itself, you see, is in obedience to God's command to believe in his beloved Son. So in that sense it is pleasing to God. But it's not faith itself that is pleasing to God, but that faith brings the soul to be united to God in Christ. Enoch had this testimony, that he pleased God, because he walked by faith, because he testified as he walked by faith. And that is what is true, right to the end of life's journey. It is true with regard to all the Old Testament saints, and it is true with regard to all the people of God in New Testament times, including those who we knew ourselves in this congregation—they died in faith. The Old Testament saints died believing that Christ was to come. The New Testament saints died in faith on the Christ who had come, when he magnified the law and made it honourable. How wonderful the faith of the Old Testament saints was! And still it is the same faith, and without this faith it is impossible to please him.

May he bless his Word.

6 Noah

HEBREWS 11:7

By faith Noah, being warned of God of things not seen as yet, moved with fear, prepared an ark to the saving of his house; by the which he condemned the world, and became heir of the righteousness which is by faith.

JANUARY 1992

WE have the Holy Spirit revealing to us here how Noah, this man of God, was warned in connection with the flood that was to engulf the generation and sweep them all away into eternity, apart from himself and his family. Noah was warned of that judgment 120 years before it happened. There were no outward signs that could be seen that could bring people to think that such a judgment would take place. Nor were there any outward signs that would lead Noah to think that such a judgment would take place. What happened was that Noah was warned of God. He came to know of the judgment that was to take place by the word of God, by the warning that he received from the word of God. He believed that word. He received that warning. As we read, he was moved with fear to the preparing of an ark to the saving of his house.

Now the deliverance that Noah experienced at that time was a deliverance with regard to a particular temporal judgment that came on the generation in which he lived. But Noah knew and understood from the same word of God that he needed a place of safety from a judgment that was to come at the end of time. The judgment that took place in the form of the flood here was a forerunner, a warning, of the judgment that is yet to come, as the destruction of Sodom and Gomorrah was also a warning of the judgment that is yet to come, when this world shall be dissolved and shall disappear in flames of fire into the nothingness from whence it came.

So Noah knew that he needed deliverance from a judgment that is not temporal but eternal. And we see the method of his deliverance from that judgment in the words, 'he became the heir of the right-eousness which is by faith.' The covenant which God made with Noah included the promise of a coming Messiah, and it was by faith in that coming Messiah and faith in the salvation that he was to work out that Noah found the true ark of salvation and a place of safety from the eternal judgment that must overtake all those who despise the Word of God and refuse to listen to the warnings of that Word.

1. Now we shall consider first of all that Noah was warned by God with regard to this judgment. And he believed the warning. During the 120 years between his receiving the warning and the judg-ment coming, he had been a preacher of righteousness. He had been preaching to his generation. He had been warning them of the judg-ment to come. And no doubt the expression that he was a preacher of righteousness means that he was also bringing before them the true ark of salvation—salvation not merely from temporal judgments but from the eternal death that is due to sin. But they ignored that, as surely as they ignored the warning with regard to the temporal judgment, which was to be the means of sending them into the eternal world and into the lake that burneth with fire and brimstone, which is the second death.

2. Then we shall consider in the second place that Noah, being warned of God, was obedient to God's warning and obedient to God's command to prepare an ark for salvation from this judgment both for himself and his family. It was a great privilege for Noah to receive the warning, but the warning could not save him. The warning did not save him. But what the warning did was, it moved him with fear to carry out the command of God with regard to securing the salvation

of himself and his family from this particular judgment. It is a great privilege for us to receive warnings of the wrath which is to come, and warnings of the certainty of perishing if we continue adding sin to sin, and warnings that we are treasuring up wrath against the day of wrath. But these warnings will not save us. The fact that we have received warnings will not save us unless we are moved by them to seek salvation.

3. Then lastly we shall notice that while Noah in his generation obtained salvation from this temporal judgment, yet he had also obtained salvation for eternity. He obtained that salvation, as we are told, through the righteousness to which he became an heir. He himself found grace in the eyes of the Lord, and that being so, he was a just man and perfect in his generation. That of course does not mean that he was without sin, but what it does mean is that he was a justified man, just like Abraham and Isaac and Jacob and like all the Old Testament saints whose faith was in the Messiah who was to come. Now we are greatly privileged, and therefore we have less excuse than these people who perished in the flood, because we have before us an ark of salvation in the person and in the work of the Lord and Saviour Jesus Christ, which we may read of, which we may pray over, which we may be led to understand. And in hiding in that ark, in believing in Christ, in coming under the shelter of the righteousness of Christ, we can find salvation for eternity. Yes, salvation for eternity! Salvation not from the wrath which was to come in 120 years, but the wrath which is to come for ever and ever and ever. What solemn words these are, 'the wrath of God'! What a solemn thought, God being angry with the wicked every day! There is fiery and holy indignation against sin in the divine being, who is your creator and mine, our lawgiver and our judge. But however solemn it is to think of that, surely this is an aspect of it which is of a particularly solemn nature, namely that it is the wrath which is to come, the wrath to which there is no end. Were you and I permitted to speak to Pharaoh, who has been under the wrath of God these thousands of years, and if we were to ask him, 'What is the most desolating experience of God's wrath? Is it the fire

that cannot be quenched? Is it the worm that gnaws incessantly at the conscience? Is it the sense of being under divine displeasure and suffering the pains of hell?' I'm sure that his answer would be, 'The most awful thing of all is that after thousands upon thousands upon thousands upon millions upon millions of years, it is still the wrath which is to come.' That's what Noah was delivered from, and that's what you and I need to be delivered from.

1. Noah was warned by God

There was Noah, in the midst of this corrupt, idolatrous generation. The 'sons of God', those who professed the true religion, were marrying the 'daughters of men', idolaters of one kind or description. That was one of the things that brought about a desolation in this generation, that the sons of God, those who were the children of Seth and professed the true religion, mingled with the world. Like Israel later on, they mingled with the heathen and learned their ways. They became corrupt, and more corrupt as the years went on. You see, the people of God are the salt of the earth. Of course, the world thinks very little of the people of God. They are very insignificant. They are not among the mighty men of renown. They are a poor and afflicted people. The world thinks very little of them. But let the world think what it likes. The fact is that the Lord's people are the salt of the earth. As long as they are here, there is an element preventing the corruption from spreading too quickly. When one of the Lord's people is taken away, in that generation, in that community, a praying voice has been silenced. The prayer in this world has been turned to praise in the eternal world, but the loss to the community, to the generation, to the congregation, to the church, is that this praying person has been taken away. Of course, if the world thinks very little of the Lord's people, it thinks even less of the idea of them praying. The value of praying people doesn't enter into the minds of the worldly. Well, let it be so, but the fact is that as long as there are praying people, there is hope for the generation, because they are the people whose prayers are ascending before the throne of God, through the golden censer, the Lord and Saviour Jesus Christ. They are praying for themselves, for their families, and for their generation, and there's no doubt that that was true of Noah too.

Now Noah's generation had reached a stage where the Lord had said, 'My Spirit shall not always strive with man.' Here is a reference to a particular activity of the Holy Spirit in the word 'to strive' with men. We are to understand by that the grace of the Holy Spirit exercised by way of restraint, what we call 'restraining grace' (and I think it's a good term) as distinct from 'saving grace'.

At the beginning, Noah's generation had enjoyed the restraining grace of the Holy Spirit. Wherever the gospel is, there is a measure of restraining grace, so that, although the heart is deceitful above all things and desperately wicked, yet as long as the Holy Spirit is exercising his restraining grace, sin does not break out in its awfulness. When God says, 'My Spirit shall not always strive with man,' this is the real reason for the outrages that take place in our day and generation—the gross, sordid immorality, the gross worldliness, the low living, the vandalism, the mugging of old women in the street, the murders, the lying, the thieving. Here is the real reason: the Holy Spirit is grieved away, not only in his converting grace, but in his restraining grace. 'My Spirit shall not always strive with man.' That is a forerunner of judgment. It is a forerunner of spiritual judgment, and it may also be, as it was in this case, a forerunner of temporal judgment.

Now in this ungodly generation was Noah, who found grace in the sight of God. Noah was an object of God's gracious love, love of which he was not worthy, because grace is love to the unworthy. He had been brought by the saving grace of the Holy Spirit to believe in the promises of God and to believe in the promised Messiah, and therefore he found grace in the eyes of God. He was a justified man. He was a righteous man, righteous in the sense that he was like Abraham—he believed God and it was counted to him for righteousness.

There he was in this wicked generation, but he was warned of God. He received a warning from God of things not seen as yet. And being a preacher of righteousness, he began to warn the generation of the coming deluge, the coming judgment. He warned them that sins that are sown have their reaping time, and in this case their sins were to have their reaping time on this side of death.

But before I go on to that, I should have mentioned something in drawing the distinction between restraining grace and converting grace (or, if you like, regenerating grace). Restraining grace just restrains, it does not change, a person's nature. Think of a leopard—if a leopard is captured and put into a cage, then it chained, it is restrained, but it is a leopard still. There's no change of nature, it does not change its spots. Under the influence of restraining grace, people may be restrained from many outward sins, and they may be constrained to do many religious duties, but there is no change of nature. Where regenerating or converting grace is, that man is a new creation. He is born again—he has a new nature, a new life, a new principle imparted to his soul. It is when these restraints are removed, where the restraining grace of the Holy Ghost is taken away, that there are great, violent outbreaks of sin and floods of iniquity. Floods of iniquity come in on a generation and a land, as was true in Noah's time. Well, if a flood of iniquity came in, there was a flood of judgment to deal with it.

Noah was warned of God. And he was warning others. But he was warning them of things not seen as yet. 'Where is the promise of his coming?' That's what the scoffers were saying, as we read in Peter. The people in Noah's generation were saying, 'This man, he's speaking about sin, he's speaking about judgment, he's speaking about a judgment that's to come, he's telling us he's been warned of God. He is a narrow minded bigot! We don't see any signs of what he's saying, that there's to be a flood to sweep the whole generation away into death and to eternity. Who would think that God would ever do such a thing?' Such things were not seen as yet. Not as yet.

But they would yet be seen. The eyes that saw Noah preaching, the ears that heard the voice of Noah warning them, these eyes were to see the flood, these ears were to hear the breaking up of the deep and the fall of the rain, and these eyes and ears were to disappear under

the flood. It's all very well to scoff, as people do nowadays, scoffing at
the idea that the wages of sin is death. They say, 'Surely God would
not do such a thing as to be angry with the wicked every day! Surely
such a thing would not happen, that a whole generation would be
swept out of time into eternity, and into a lost eternity, by the judgment of God!' People scoff at the idea of the wrath of God, the judgment of God.

2. Noah was obedient to God's warning

Noah was saying he'd been warned of God, but he was speaking of
something they could not see any evidences of. There he is, building
an ark. No sign of water. What's he doing? He's speaking about something that's to come. He's speaking about something that is not seen
as yet. You see, this is the great point. Noah believed the warning. He
believed the warning because it was the word of God. He did not
reach this conclusion by any kind of logical form of reasoning based
on evidence that he could see, but he was warned of God. The word
of God was what warned him, and he believed the word of God when
God spoke of things not seen as yet. He believed that.

Very closely bound up with that belief was this, that Noah
believed that God was just in this judgment. He believed with regard
to this warning, as surely as David believed with regard to his own sin,
that God was just when he judges, and clear when he speaks. Noah
was quite clearly convinced that this judgment was an exercise of the
glorious attribute of divine justice, and that the sins of that generation
were altogether worthy of this divine judgment.

It is essential to faith to recognise that God is just when he
condemns sin to eternal death, when he condemns *my* sin to eternal
death. When you get people who are trying to slip away from that
conception of the glory of God, namely the inflexibility of his justice
in punishing sin, that is a sign that they are unconverted. Noah was a
changed man, and it's an element in the saving change that overtakes
all God's people that they see clearly and unmistakeably and accept
that God is just when he condemns their sins. As the psalmist says, 'If
thou, Lord, shouldst mark iniquities, O Lord, who could stand?' Who

can stand if thou wilt mark iniquity? This is part of the glory of the judge of all the earth, and part of the glory that sinners are to see when God will come to judge the world in righteousness, 'justice to give each one' (Psalm 9:8). You and I must each come to this. Noah came to it. He preached to them here, being warned of God of things not seen as yet. He knew that this would be fulfilled, because it was part of the justice of God, and because it was bound up with God's holy indignation and wrath against sin.

Noah warned them of things not seen as yet. That's what the warnings of God's Word are connected with—warnings of the wrath which is to come. It is not seen as yet. It was seen in a partial way in this temporal judgment, and it was seen at the overthrow of Sodom and Gomorrah, and it is seen in many ways in the history of the world. But that is not what we are dependent on. What we depend on is that it is the Word of God. It is a warning from God. That the wages of sin is death. Sin will be followed by judgment.

And therefore there is a necessity for being prepared. There was a necessity for being prepared for that temporal judgment, the flood, and Noah was moved with fear to prepare. Not with slavish fear, but with reverential awe at the judgment of God, and a realisation that if he was to be delivered from this temporal judgment he would need to prepare for it.

Now every one of you must agree, and your consciences must agree, that you have been warned. You have been warned about sin. You have been warned of what the Saviour said, 'Except ye believe that I am he, ye shall die in your sins.' But it is not enough that you have been warned. The warning will not save you. It was not what was meant to save Noah, and it did not save Noah. But it did move him. He was moved to be obedient to God, to prepare the ark to the saving of himself and his house. You cannot deny it, you know very well in your own conscience before God, that you have been warned of the wrath which is to come. But the question that you must face, each one of you, is, have you been moved? Have you been moved? All these warnings you have been hearing, have they moved you to seek preparation? Have they moved you to seek salvation? Or are you like the people in Noah's time, you do not believe it? It is not seen! The wrath of God is not seen! But remember this, it is not seen *as yet*.

The years were passing. Noah was preaching, warning. Ten years pass. 'Where is the sign of his coming? Where's the flood?' Another fifty years. A century. 'Where's the sign of his coming?' That's what the scoffers were saying. What about yourselves? Year after year after year. It's now thirty-one or thirty-two years since I came here, and you know very well that you've been warned during these years, and now are you saying, 'What of it?' Well, you have been spared till now. You have not entered into the wrath of God, you have not gone to death and to eternity, nor as an overflowing flood has your soul been carried away into the lake that burneth with fire and brimstone. That has not happened—as yet. As yet. But be assured that it will happen, if you are not moved to seek, and to prepare, to find a hiding place from the storm of God's wrath.

3. Noah obtained salvation for eternity

Noah was obedient with regard to this temporal judgment. But it was far more important for him that he was obedient with the obedience of faith. So he became a justified man, a righteous man. He became one who walked with God. He was reconciled to God. He walked in the light as God was in the light, and he had fellowship with God. Moved with fear, he had come to the obedience of faith. He had come to find an ark of safety of far greater value, of far greater glory, of far greater import, than the ark that he built with his own hands according to God's command. For we read that he was an heir of the righteousness which is by faith. Noah believed in the Messiah that was to come, just as surely as Abraham, Isaac and Jacob did, and just as surely as Jeremiah did. Jeremiah spoke of this Messiah in these words, 'Jehovah Tsidkenu'—'the Lord our righteousness'. This is the ark in which the soul is to obtain salvation from eternal wrath, the ark in which the soul is to obtain eternal salvation—under the shelter of the righteousness of Christ.

Now the ark which Noah built was made of gopher wood. But the ark that Noah was looking to by faith for the salvation of his soul was a glorious ark, because this ark was a person. They had been told at the beginning that this person was the seed of the woman. Then Scripture unfolds and makes known that the seed of the woman was in his own person the eternal Son of the Father in truth and love, God in the second person, the brightness of the Father's glory and the express image of his person. It also makes known that he came to dwell in a holy humanity, and in that holy humanity to work out salvation by his obedience unto death.

Now the garment of Christ's righteousness is a garment without seam, but for the sake of understanding it we refer to the obedience of Christ with regard to his righteousness on the one hand as 'active' obedience. By 'active obedience' we mean obedience to the law of God in the room and place of the guilty. That obedience to the law of God was necessary to secure life. The man that doeth these things shall live by them—life was to be obtained by obedience to the law. And since the Saviour knew that his people could never obtain life in that way, he came in the fulness of the times, born of a woman, made under the law, to obey the law in their room and place and to obtain the life so found. The man that doeth these things, the man that renders obedience to the law of God shall obtain life by that law.

Then the other part of the righteousness of Christ we call his 'passive' obedience. By that we mean his obedience in his passion, his suffering—his obedience as the Lamb of God bearing the sins of his people in his own body on the tree and suffering the death due to these sins. That suffering, the Saviour tells us, was like a flood. 'Save me, O God,' he said, 'because the floods / do so environ me, / that even unto my very soul / come in the waters be.' The floods of judgment, the wrath of God, entered into his very soul. But he was able to make an end of that by his sufferings unto death. Therefore his active and his passive obedience together form a righteousness which, when the soul is enclosed in it, makes an ark for that soul, and the law and justice of God have no claims against him. On the contrary, the law and justice of God secure that he should obtain the life that shall never end.

So this is the ark of salvation that Noah was looking to for eternity. He was looking to the ark of gopher wood for time, for this coming judgment. But when he was looking to the eternal world, when he was looking to the things not seen as yet—to eternity, to the judgment and justice of God in the eternal world, against his sins—then Christ and his righteousness was the ark into which he fled in the obedience of faith. He believed God, he believed that God was to supply a Saviour, and he believed that that Saviour would work out salvation. That was the ark which he was in for eternity. That is the ark in which he became the heir and the possessor of the righteousness which is by faith. Clothed in that righteousness he walked with God in this world, and clothed in that righteousness he was a preacher of the everlasting gospel.

Now, what about yourself? Have you been moved with fear that your sins would bring you to eternal death? And have you been moved with fear by the warning of God that the soul that sinneth, it shall die? And have you come to view by faith the righteousness of Christ? Have you come to view by faith Christ as the righteousness of your soul, the Saviour of the lost and the undone? And have you obeyed? Noah obeyed God. Have you obeyed the call of the everlasting gospel to flee to this ark, to flee from the wrath which is to come, to flee to Christ Jesus, the ark where there is eternal salvation? Do you know anything of what they knew in Thessalonica? 'They themselves show of us what manner of entering we had unto you when we came with the gospel to you, how you turned to God from idols, to serve the living God, to wait for his Son from heaven, whom he raised from the dead, even Jesus, which delivered us from the wrath which is to come.' Jesus delivers us from the wrath which is to come.

Therefore I put the question to you again. Have the warnings you heard been blessed to your soul, to move you to flee from the wrath which is to come? To move you to turn from your sins to God? To move you to obey the Scripture that says, from the mouth of God,

'Let the wicked forsake his way, and the unrighteous man his thoughts, and let him return unto the Lord, and he will have mercy upon him, and to our God, and he will abundantly pardon'? And have you been moved to close in with Christ in the everlasting gospel, to rest on the righteousness of Christ as your hope for eternity? And if that is so, then, clothed in this righteousness, you're safer than Noah was when God shut the door of the ark. Noah was safe there in the ark on the top of the floods until the floods subsided. He was safe there from that temporal judgment. But those who by faith have closed in with Christ in the everlasting gospel, and who have come like Noah to be justified by faith, to be clothed in the righteousness of Christ—they're in a place of safety from the wrath which is to come. They are safe for time and they are safe for eternity.

We are also told that as Noah was moved with fear, and as he prepared the ark to the saving of the house, he condemned the world. He was warning them in his preaching, that's true, but he 'condemned the world' in the sense that he believed the warning of God and they didn't. Wherever there is a child of God, who has come like Noah to be moved with fear to seek salvation, and who has found salvation in Christ and his righteousness, they are now walking with God, in fellowship with God, and taking the side of God against the world. They are testifying to the world of the wrath which is to come, of the justice of God—yes, and of the mercy of God, and of the grace of God, and the righteousness of Christ—that Christ is the one name given under heaven among men whereby they can be saved!

You see, that is the contest today. The true Christian is condemning those who expect to be saved by the Virgin Mary. He is condemning those who expect to be saved by Buddha. He is condemning those who expect to be saved by the gods of the Hindus. He is condemning those who expect to be saved without being born again. True Christians condemn the world. That's why the world hates them. That's why the world tries to cover them with scorn. You know what they say. 'These Christians think they're the only people who are right and everybody else is wrong.' Well, Noah was right, and everybody else was wrong. They discovered that under the waves of the deluge, when their souls were in the lake of fire.

Noah condemned the world. This is inevitable, because he walked with God. The same thing was true of Enoch. Enoch walked with God, and 'he was not', they could not find him. As you know, Enoch was what we might call a preacher of the law. He was giving warnings, and by these warnings and his conduct he walked with God. He could not be found, because God translated him. I believe that that means that when his enemies went to destroy him, God translated him. That does not happen to all the people of God. Many of them are put to death by their enemies, like Stephen, who was stoned. But, you see, when Stephen was stoned, he got a view of something that was to come. He got a view of Christ in his glory, and death meant very little to him then. So it was true of Noah. And so it will be true of all the people of God. Whatever fears they may have about death—and they do have fears—the Lord will see to it that they'll get views of Christ that will take the sting out of death for them. And then the scorn of the world and the mockery of the world will mean very little to them.

But that is not what's important just now. What is important for you is this: Noah, being warned of God, was moved with fear, and obeyed the word of God with regard to salvation both from this temporal judgment and from eternal judgment. The question for you and for me is, have we been so moved? The warnings have come to us, we cannot deny it. We all know it perfectly well. But have we been moved with fear? Or are we just saying, 'Well, that's something that we have not seen.' But remember, my dear friend, it is true that these things are not seen, but they are not seen *as yet*. Noah's generation did not see the flood while Noah was warning them of it, but they saw it in due time. And so all those who despise the warnings of the Word of God, who neglect the great salvation, must endure the wrath of God. The Scripture says so plainly, clearly, unmistakeably.

'How shall we escape, if we neglect so great salvation?' There is no escape.

May he bless his Word

7 Abraham

HEBREWS 11:8–10
*By faith Abraham, when he was called to go out into a place
which he should after receive for an inheritance, obeyed; and
he went out, not knowing whither he went. By faith he
sojourned in the land of promise, as in a strange country,
dwelling in tabernacles with Isaac and Jacob, the heirs with
him of the same promise: for he looked for a city which hath
foundations, whose builder and maker is God.*

WEDNESDAY, 28ᵀᴴ FEBRUARY 1984

A S we saw in the case of Noah, and the others of whom we read
in this chapter of the Word of God, they were all possessors of
the grace of faith. That faith which is the gift of God had been wrought
in their hearts by the Holy Spirit. The Holy Spirit through the apostle
Paul in this chapter here indicates the nature of the grace of faith and
the various fruits which are bound up with the exercise of that grace
in the souls of God's people in this world. We must always remember
that the grace of faith—like all the graces of the Holy Spirit—is an
exercise of soul. Here we are told with regard to Abraham, as we were
formerly told with regard to Noah, how his soul was exercised in
connection with his possessing the grace of faith.

Abraham was called
The first thing that we notice with regard to the grace of faith is that
it has an exercise in connection with the call of God. Abraham 'was
called to go out to a place which he should afterward receive for an

inheritance'. His faith, and the exercise of his faith, was connected with the call of God. So it is true in New Testament times as it was in Old Testament times that faith is wrought in the heart of a sinner by the Spirit of God in connection with effectual calling. In connection with the call of God the Holy Spirit grants the grace of faith and its fruits which we have brought before us here.

This call of God came to Abraham when he was in Ur of the Chaldees—when he was an idolater. This call did not come to him because he sought it. He did not seek it. He was sunk in the darkness and the ignorance and the enmity to God of idolatrous worship. Some believe, because his name includes the word for 'father', that he was a prominent priest in the worship of idols. In any case, one thing is certain: he was a worshipper of false gods when this call came to him. And that indicates this point, that the call came to him not because of anything good in him, for there was nothing good in him.

Abraham was a sinner, and he demonstrated and made it clear and plain that he was a sinner by living in the darkness of idolatry, in a place where they worshipped the gods which are idols dumb, which blinded nations fear, and where they lived contravening the second commandment, that they were not to worship God by idols. He was sunk in that darkness, the darkness of idolatrous worship. That darkness embraces the darkness of the ignorance of God, for God is a Spirit, and he cannot be worshipped through sticks and stones, he cannot be worshipped by idols. Abraham, as he was sunk in the desolations of idolatry, as is true of idolaters to the present day, was one in whom darkness reigned, the darkness of the ignorance of God.

And yet this call came to Abraham. It came to Abraham in the free grace of God. It came to Abraham by God's choice, not by Abraham's choice. In the free grace of God, this call came to a man who was a sinner living in idolatry, in whom no good dwelt.

Now, Stephen says with regard to this call that 'the God of our fathers appeared unto Abraham'. The God of glory appeared to Abraham, and it was this that rendered the call effectual in Abraham's experience. God appeared in this call. Light came into his soul with respect to this call, such that when the call came to him, he obeyed. As we were reading in the book of Genesis, God addressed him, in his soul and in his conscience, addressing him with authority and with divine power. So that when the Lord said to Abraham, 'Get thee out of thy country and from thy kindred and from thy father's house,' Abraham felt with these words an authority and power that he never felt in his life before—the authority and power of God. A conviction was wrought in his heart that the one who spoke to him was the God of eternity. This light was secretly let into his soul by the power of the Holy Ghost, that the one who was speaking to him was the Lord, the God of eternity. Where the word of a king is, there is power, and where the word of the King of kings is, the word of 'the King eternal, immortal, invisible, and the only wise God', authority is felt with it when it comes into the soul of any sinner.

As surely as Abraham felt it in his own day and generation, thousands of years ago, so any sinner feeling the authority of this Word under the effectual calling of the Holy Spirit feels that God is speaking to him or to her in this Word—that it is not the word of men but the Word of God. That is why all God's people have such reverence for the Word of God, such care and concern about the Word of God. And that is why they do not believe that those who deny God's Word or who trifle with the Word of God have the grace of faith at all, or that they ever felt in their own experience this divine authority and power with the Word of God. So when the Lord comes to call a sinner today, as surely as when he came to call Abraham back in his age and generation, he does so by his Word, and by letting into the soul who is hearing the Word of God sufficient light to convince that soul that God is speaking to him or her.

Abraham was called to go out

This call involves departing. That's what it involved for Abraham—it was a call to depart. And so it ever will be. A call coming to a sinner is a call to that sinner to depart from his sins. It was a call to Abraham to get out from his country and his kindred and his father's house. All these things are natural ties of great strength and power, and they were undoubtedly so in the case of Abraham. But his country was the land of idolatry, the place of ignorance of God, the place of enmity against God, the place of spiritual darkness, and when this call came to him it was a call to him to forsake the foolish and live.

It was similar to the call that we read of in Psalm 45, 'O daughter, hearken and regard, / and do thine ear incline; / likewise forget thy father's house / and people that are thine.' It was the same call that came to Ruth, the Moabitish damsel down in the darkness of the land of Moab. It is the same call that comes to sinners still in our day and generation. When God is pleased to call a sinner effectually by his grace, that sinner is called on to depart from his sins. 'Let the wicked forsake his way, and the unrighteous man his thoughts; and let him return unto the Lord, and he will have mercy upon him, and to our God, for he will abundantly pardon.' It is a call to turn one's back on sin and idolatry and darkness and ignorance and serving diverse lusts and pleasures. It is a call to forsake the foolish, and live.

Abraham obeyed

And Abraham showed that the Holy Spirit was working in his soul, and working the grace of faith in his soul, in that he obeyed. 'By faith Abraham, when he was called to go out into a place which he should after receive for an inheritance, obeyed; and he went out.'

This call came to him. It was an irresistible call, it was an invincible call, it was a call in the power and grace of the Spirit of God. It was a calling on him to forsake his darkness, his idolatry, his idols and all that pertained to the land of idolatry in Ur of the Chaldees. And Abraham obeyed.

He believed that it was the word of God, and he believed that it was God who was commanding him to forsake his sins, to forsake the foolish, and live, and he obeyed. So it ever will be. If you and I ever hear this call, it will be a call to us as sinners to forsake our sins, to turn our back on them, and where this call is effectual, we will obey. When this call comes, we will obey, and we will be found forsaking our evil ways—forsaking our sins, our Sabbath-breaking, our going to the vanities of this world, the dances and the discos, and our indulgence in all the pleasures of sin, which are but for a season. It is one of the delusions of the present generation, that a person can be a Christian and still be in the world, enjoying the pleasures and comforts of the world. That is a delusion. That is something that people can only believe if they never felt what Abraham felt, and if we do not feel what Abraham felt then we will not be with Abraham in eternity.

But Abraham felt this call in his soul's experience, and he felt called on to forsake his country, his kindred, his father's house, and we read here that 'he went out, not knowing whither he went'. What he did know and understand, and it was clear to him, as clear as the sun in the noonday sky, was that he was to leave Ur of the Chaldees—he was to leave the place of sin, and the place of sinning. He went out from that place, not knowing whither he went, but knowing one thing—that he would have to obey the word of God. He was now disposed to obey the word of God wherever the word of God would lead him, as the Lord himself had promised he would lead him into a land that he would show him.

Abraham was given an inheritance

And that was a land which was afterward to be given to him for an inheritance, as we read here. 'He was called to go out into a place which he should after receive for an inheritance.' This was opened up to his soul when he obeyed, when he went out not knowing whither he went. All he knew was that he was going out to an inheritance that God would show him.

There was a sense in which that inheritance was the land of Canaan, but it is also clear that there is more than the land of Canaan embraced in that inheritance. As we read in Genesis, God's promise to Abraham was not only the promise of the land but also the promise of the seed. 'I will bless thee, and I will make thy name great; and I will bless them that bless thee, and in thee shall all the families of the earth be blessed.' That was part of the inheritance—there was a land, and there was also the seed promised, and that seed, Paul tells us, was Christ. So when Abraham was called to go out to this inheritance, it was an inheritance that was bound up with the promise of God, in connection with the Messiah who was to come, the New Testament Isaac who was to come. And he embraced that, and he looked forward to this promise. As the Saviour himself said, 'Abraham saw my day and was glad.' Abraham was glad that he saw this inheritance that he so greatly needed in the Messiah, in the one that was to come, in the Saviour of God's providing. This Saviour would be born eventually in the Promised Land in Bethlehem, the house of bread. He said himself, 'I am the bread of life,' and he exhorted sinners while he was in the world, 'Labour not for the meat which perisheth, but for the meat that endureth unto eternal life.' Abraham's inheritance was the inheritance bound up with the Saviour—or, in other words, it was the inheritance of salvation through the Saviour of God's appointment.

Now, as far as the light of revelation is concerned, we have clearer light on that Saviour and on that salvation than Abraham ever had. He had a degree of light, and that degree of light was all that was necessary to give him saving faith. But in the Word of God, in the Gospels and in the Epistles and so on, we have great light given to us on the great Saviour and the great salvation. We have great light on the seed that was born in the land of promise, in Bethlehem. That seed was Christ, says Paul—the promise was not 'to seeds', as of many, but 'to thy seed', as of one, and that seed was Christ, the Son of God. He was the Son of God in our nature, who in the fulness of times worked out salvation for those who by nature are in spiritual darkness, full of sin and full of iniquity, who are the children of wrath, even as others. The Saviour came in God's great name to save—to die the death which divine justice required him to die, on the cross of Calvary, in the room and place of the guilty, a number that no man can number of the human race. In him there is eternal salvation for the very chief of sinners.

This is the great inheritance which every sinner should desire to possess. Every sinner should desire to be able to say with David, in Psalm 16, where he mentions God as 'of mine inheritance and cup the portion'. *God* was David's inheritance, and God was ultimately Abraham's inheritance. And the God who was David's and Abraham's inheritance was God in Christ, God revealed in Christ, God who was in Christ reconciling the world unto himself, not imputing their trespasses unto them, God who provided the Saviour whose blood was shed for the remission of the sins of many.

And although Abraham saw this afar off, nevertheless he embraced it. As we read later on in this chapter, all the Old Testament saints embraced these promises, and they embraced in particular the promise with regard to the seed—the seed who was eventually to be born in the land of Canaan, the seed who was eventually to be born in the town of Bethlehem, the seed who was eventually to be crucified outside the city of the great king as the New Testament Isaac. The Old Testament Isaac was about to be sacrificed on Mount Moriah, but the New Testament Isaac was sacrificed on Mount Calvary, the place of a skull.

This is the inheritance to which Abraham was called, and he went out. He did not know whither he was going, certainly as far as the land was concerned, but neither did he know much of the spiritual inheritance, until it was revealed and made known to him more and more. Yet he saw and understood that this was his inheritance—the God of eternity in the person of his beloved Son, the Saviour who would come in God's great name to save. He went out not knowing whither he went, but one thing he did know was that if he followed the word of God he would find this inheritance.

And so you may be assured. If you feel your sins and your iniquities, and feel that God is calling you away from the land of sin and the land of darkness, then you may be sure that if you will follow the Word of God, the Word of God will lead you to Christ who said himself, 'Search the Scriptures, for in them you think that you have eternal life, and they are they which speak of me.' You can be assured on this point, that if you will follow the Word of God and the teachings of God's Word, however much you may feel your own ignorance now, the Lord is able to enlighten you and will enlighten you, so that you will come to embrace this inheritance in the promise of the everlasting gospel. That is where Christ is to be found—he is to be found in the promise of the everlasting gospel. We need not ascend into heaven nor go down into the depths, but the word is nigh thee, even in thy mouth, and in thy heart, that is, the word of faith, which we preach. In the everlasting gospel Christ is held forth, without money and without price, to poor, dark, empty, blind, hell-deserving, condemned sinners, to be their inheritance. The wages of sin is death, but the gift of God is eternal life through Jesus Christ our Lord. Abraham followed the Word of God, and that is what you must do too.

Abraham sojourned in the land of promise

We also read that Abraham sojourned in the land of promise. 'By faith he sojourned in the land of promise, as in a strange country.'

This demonstrates what I have already been saying—that the inheritance was not the land of promise itself, because when Abraham came into the land of Canaan he only *sojourned* in the land of promise—and 'as in a strange country'. Canaan wasn't his home, it wasn't his rest. In fact, as far as Abraham was concerned, all he ever possessed of that promised land was the grave in Machpelah where he laid Sarah first of all and then he was laid there himself. Rather, he sojourned in this land—he was sojourning there on his way to the fuller inheritance that he was to possess. Although he was in the land of Canaan, and whilst it was to be given as a possession to his seed— historically that was to be done in due time—that's not the important part of the inheritance, for what Abraham's faith fed on was the inheritance that was promised in Christ, the inheritance of eternal salvation, behind and beyond this world and beyond the land of Canaan. As we read here, he was journeying to 'a city that hath foundations, whose builder and maker is God'. So he sojourned in the land of promise and he was a stranger in that land. The land was filled with the tribes of Canaan—the Hivites and the Hittites and all those heathenish tribes. Abraham was a stranger among them. He was in the land of Canaan but he was not of it. And so God's people who have this faith that Abraham had, and this embracing of the promise of God, as the Saviour himself said, they are in the world but they are not of it—they are not of the world, they are strangers in the world, and they are sojourners in the world, because this is not their rest.

Now Abraham was not sojourning alone. 'He sojourned in the land of promise, as in a strange country, dwelling in tabernacles with Isaac and Jacob, the heirs with him of the same promise.' They were in tabernacles, which were temporary and would eventually fall to the ground, in contradistinction to the inheritance they were ultimately to have in the city whose builder and maker is God. In these tabernacles Abraham had companions, and they were heirs with him of the same promise. They had the same precious faith, they were sojourning with him, they were saying with respect to the land of Canaan, 'This is not our rest,' but they were looking for the rest that remaineth to the people of God.

So the people of God journey together in this world. They don't have any friends in the world and they don't wish to have any. But they do have friends among the people of God. Abraham didn't want to have anything to do with the Hittites or the Hivites or the Amorites or any of the Canaanitish tribes with all their dark idolatry, out of which he had been delivered. But he did rejoice in the fellowship of Isaac and of Jacob. They dwelt in tabernacles together, he was at home with Isaac and Jacob—he enjoyed their company, he enjoyed their fellowship as they were journeying Zion-ward. 'So they from strength unwearied go / still forward unto strength, / until in Zion they appear / before the Lord at length' (Psalm 84:7). As they journeyed together, they had fellowship and communion with one another with regard to their sojourning, with regard to the promise of God, with regard to how God had called them, with regard to the preciousness of the Word of God, with regard to the preciousness of the Messiah who was to come and who would fulfil the purposes of God. And so it is in this world. Even in this bleak, desolate, evil and adulterous generation in which you and I live, there are still a few of the people of God, and they should be keeping close together as they are journeying Zion-ward, encouraging one another, in fellowship with one another.

The same thing was true with regard to Ruth, the Moabitish damsel. She journeyed from the land of Moab to the land of Judah in the company of Naomi, and her mind was that she would cleave to Naomi, and she did cleave to her. Orpah turned back—she wept, but they were not the tears of real love. She went back to the land of Moab and back to the young men and the young women and the enjoyments of Moab. But not Ruth. Her language was, 'Intreat me not to leave thee, or to return from following after thee: for whither thou goest, I will go; and where thou lodgest, I will lodge: thy people shall be my people, and thy God my God: where thou diest, will I die, and there will I be buried.' I think that if you could have been listening behind the tents where Abraham and Isaac and Jacob dwelt, you would find them all saying the same—they were journeying together and they did not want to leave one another, but they were journeying together Zion-ward, on their way to the inheritance that is incorruptible and undefiled, and that shall never fade away, reserved for those who are kept by the power of God through faith unto salvation.

As I have already hinted, wherever the grace of faith is, it is evidenced by obedience to the Word of God when we sojourn in the land of promise. That is the outstanding lesson in the case of Abraham here, and Paul, in writing by the Spirit of God to the Hebrews, was putting this example before them. They were meeting with trials and tribulations, and they were to understand clearly that where the grace of faith was, it would evidence itself in obedience to the Word of God.

Abraham looked for a city

They were sojourners in the land of promise and dwelling in tabernacles, 'for they looked for a city that hath foundations, whose builder and maker is God.

This city is described in another phrase by the Saviour when he says, 'In my Father's house are many mansions: if it were not so, I would have told you. I go to prepare a place for you. And if I go and prepare a place for you, I will come again, and receive you unto myself; that where I am, there ye may be also.'

This is what they looked for—a city that had foundations, whose builder and whose maker was God. It was not like the tabernacles they were dwelling in which were merely temporary. Neither was it like the city of Jerusalem, which was eventually to be built in the land of Canaan, wonderfully built though it was. Even Jerusalem was not to be compared with the city they looked for—Jerusalem's foundations were razed to the ground by its enemies. But this is a city that has foundations, whose builder and maker is God.

'Builder' and 'maker' of course emphasise the same concept, that heaven is a place in the universe of God which God has prepared, and it has foundations—foundations laid by God, and in particular foundations laid by God in his eternal purpose. Heaven is the place where his glory is manifested in a special way. And he will bring into this heaven a number which no man can number of the lost and the ruined race to which you and I belong. The foundation was laid in the purposes of his everlasting love, as a foundation that will never be shaken, world without end. God is the builder, he is the maker, he is the one who has planned it, he is the one who has built it, this place in the universe of God where his glory is manifested in a special way. This is the city to which Abraham was journeying, and that's the city where his soul is now, and the souls of Isaac and Jacob along with him, and David and Samuel and Jephthae, and all the others who are mentioned in this chapter. As to their souls they are all now in this city, the city of the New Jerusalem, the city of heaven, the city where the Lamb is in the midst of the throne, where the glory of God shines throughout that city, and where the love of God is enjoyed by all the inhabitants of the city, where they shall never say they are sick, and where sorrow and sighing is forever passed away.

So it is with regard to all the people of God. They may have many trials and difficulties in this world, and these are appointed for them—Christ has told them in his Word, 'Ye shall have tribulation, but be of good cheer: I have overcome the world.' We are told that those who will be in this city will have white robes and the palms of victory in their hand, for they are those who have come out of great tribulation, who have washed their robes and made them white in the blood of the Lamb. But in this world their faith is in the promise of God, that they shall be with Christ, which, as Paul says, is far better. 'For to me to live is Christ,' he said, 'and to die is gain.' He said that, you remember, when he was in prison, and when it looked like he was to be put to death in the prison—that was one alternative. The other alternative was to be set free and live. So that for him to live was Christ, but to die would be gain, because his soul would go to the city that hath foundations, whose builder and maker is God.

So Abraham's journey began from Ur of the Chaldees, and it was to end in everlasting glory. As that was true of Abraham and Isaac and Jacob, so it will be true of all God's people in this generation in which you and I live. And therefore we should seek to ensure that we have this precious faith by which we discern the things of the Spirit of God, for eye hath not seen, nor ear heard, neither have entered into the heart of man, the things which God hath prepared for them that love him, but God has revealed them unto us by his Spirit. And in revealing them to us by his Spirit he reveals them to the grace of faith, to the eye of faith, so that they behold the unsearchable riches of Christ, and beyond that the inheritance that is incorruptible and undefiled and that shall never fade away, world without end. We should, each one of us, seek above all things that we too may be on our way to Zion with our faces thitherward.

May he bless his Word.

8 Sarah

HEBREWS 11:11–13

*Through faith also Sara herself received strength to conceive
seed, and was delivered of a child when she was past age,
because she judged him faithful who had promised. Therefore sprang there even of one, and him as good as dead, so
many as the stars of the sky in multitude, and as the sand
which is by the sea shore innumerable.*

WEDNESDAY, 7TH MARCH 1984

WE were endeavouring on the last occasion to consider the case
of Abraham, whom the apostle Paul brings before the
Hebrews as one of those who lived a life of faith on the Son of God.
He had spoken of Abel and of Enoch and of Noah before that, and
now he comes to speak of Sarah. No doubt among other reasons he
did so to make it plain that the grace of faith does not apply to men
only—the exploits involved in connection with the possession and the
exercise of the grace of faith belong to women as well as to men. Sarah
was an heir of promise like Abraham, she was a like partaker of the
same precious faith as he had, and we exercise that same faith.

I have been endeavouring to emphasise that the grace of faith
needs and must have the promise of God. If the grace of faith does not
have the promise of God, then the grace of faith has nothing. The
grace of faith is the empty hand of the soul that is filled with the
promise of God, but if the promise of God is not there, then the hand
of faith remains empty. It was true with regard to Sarah, as it was true

with regard to Abraham, that the Lord gave her a promise. He gave her a promise that she would have a child long after that would be expected according to the course of nature. The words 'when she was past age' indicate that to be the case. It was through faith that she received the strength for this remarkable event to take place. Therefore, as always, we must view the promise of God when we come to speak of the grace of faith, because that is what the grace of faith itself always does. The grace of faith is empty unless it has a hold of the promise of God.

Now I already elaborated on this in the case of Abraham (and of course it is true with regard to all), that the grace of faith is wrought in connection with the call of God. That is very important. The grace of faith is not something that is spun out of the bosom of the person himself or herself. The faith that is spoken of here is the gift of God. It is wrought in the heart by the Holy Ghost, in connection with the call of God being made effectual. We do not have an explanation given us, as we have in the case of Abraham, of how Sarah came to have the grace of faith, but the Scriptures tell us quite plainly here that she did have the grace of faith.

The promise which Sarah was given

The promise of God to Sarah was that she would have a child when she was past age. When she received that promise, you remember that first of all her faith stumbled. And that teaches us that, even where the grace of faith exists in reality and in truth, as it was here, there may be stumblings, maybe with regard to the difficulties that arise in connection with the question of how the promise of God is going to be fulfilled, whatever the nature of that promise may be.

Not only did Sarah herself stumble, but Abraham did too. Sarah laughed within herself, saying, 'After I am waxed old shall I have pleasure, my lord being old also?' (Genesis 18:12). She was not alone in that. We must also remember that Abraham fell on his face, and laughed, and said in his heart, 'Shall a child be born unto him that is an hundred years old? And shall Sarah, that is ninety years old, bear?'

(Genesis 17:17). So in the case of them both there was a stumbling when the promise was given as to how that promise was to be fulfilled.

That is very often the case. There are difficulties associated with the promise of God which cause faith to stumble. And of course the stumbling of faith is accentuated by the power of unbelief because it is in the nature of unbelief to contemplate and take into account all the difficulties that arise in connection with the possibility of the promise of God being fulfilled. But it is no evidence that we do not have true faith, just because we are harassed by unbelief. On the contrary, I am of the opinion that it is much more likely to indicate that the faith is real when it is troubled with unbelief, because unbelief belongs to the old nature, which wars against the new nature. And we therefore expect that wherever there is the grace of faith in the new nature, the sin of unbelief will be in the sinful nature, and that unbelief will be rising in the soul in which the grace of faith is, and will seek to cause the grace of faith to stumble. We should not think that our faith is not genuine just because on occasions our faith is so affected by unbelief that we stumble. It is the case that on occasions our faith is so affected by unbelief that we stumble. Sarah's faith was genuine. But this part of the Word of God shows us that when the promise of God is given, there may be circumstances which arise which cause the grace of faith to stumble.

'Sarah laughed within herself, saying, After I am waxed old shall I have pleasure, my lord being old also?' These were very real difficulties, most serious difficulties. And faith is not in any way like an ostrich that digs its head in the sand and pays no attention to realities. On the contrary, faith is very conscious of the realities, for the simple reason that the grace of faith is desirous that the promise should be fulfilled, for the promise is precious to the grace of faith. It was a great promise and a precious promise to Sarah that she would have this child, as it was also to Abraham, but there were grave, serious, real difficulties in connection with that particular matter, with regard to both Abraham and Sarah. They were both old and stricken in age, and the natural process in connection with their physical condition had reached the stage when, without some very remarkable event taking place, the promise just could not be fulfilled.

Now you must remember that Sarah was barren up to this time. She had been barren during the whole of their married life, and now here was the Lord saying that she was going to have this child, when all expectation of having children was past. The time for childbearing had passed both as far as Sarah was concerned and also, for all that they could see, as far as Abraham was concerned too. So Sarah's faith was faced with this real, serious difficulty—one that she was supremely conscious of, one that she could not ignore, one that could not be passed by, one that could not be lost in some fog of some kind or other. This was a stark reality standing out—she was waxed old, she had had no children up to this time, the time for childbearing had passed, then surely she would wonder, 'Shall I have pleasure, my lord being old also?' According to the course of nature, according to all the evidences of nature, all these evidences were contrary to the promise of God. They were standing in the way of the promise of God being fulfilled.

Therefore her faith stumbled. The evidence of these realities, which were going contrary to the fulfilment of the promise, were so weighty in the case of Sarah that her faith stumbled, although her faith was genuine. You see, true religion is a living thing. It is not some kind of mathematical formula that people just apply and it works out. It is not something that goes into a computer and it comes out all right at the end. Faith is a living thing. And like all life it meets with resistance and it meets with difficulties, and it meets with trials. But the pressures of these difficulties and the stumbling of Sarah's faith in connection with these difficulties did not mean her faith was not genuine. But it did mean that her faith needed light and her faith needed strength in order that her faith would close in with the promise and that her expectation of the promise being fulfilled would be strong. That is the next point that the apostle deals with in connection with the faith of Sarah.

Sarah judged him faithful who had promised

How did Sarah overcome these real, genuine difficulties with which her faith was confronted? Well, we are told how this happened: 'she judged him faithful who had promised.' That was the way she got strength, and that was the way she got light, to encourage her in connection with the promise.

That strength and light was given her by the Lord in the words that he used when he said to her, 'Is anything too hard for the Lord?' When we come to a promise, what the promise contains is one thing, but the important thing is that *God* is in the promise. It is the promise of God. It is not a promise of a man, the promise of another fellow human being, but it is a promise of God. It is important not only as to what the promise is, but the fact that God is in the promise. Therefore in considering the promise we are not merely to consider what is in the promise—and consider consequently the difficulties which arise in connection with its fulfilment—but we must consider that God is in the promise. That is exactly what happened in the case of Sarah. She had the promise given to her, but she saw that God was in this promise—it was the promise of *God*. This is how her faith overcame, because 'she judged *him* faithful who had promised'.

If we look at the context of what happened, there are two views given us of God in connection with the promise, and both these views are of great importance in order that we should have comfort and consolation with regard to such promises as we may receive by faith. The first is, as I mentioned, that the Lord said to her, 'Is there anything too hard for the Lord?' This view was presented to her, that God was in the promise in all his power. There was nothing too hard for the Lord. The things which are impossible with men are possible with God, because he is the one of infinite power, because he is the almighty God of Jacob, and because he is the almighty one in whom is everlasting strength and everlasting power. Therefore, however hard it may seem to the soul to think that the promise is going to be fulfilled, this is the answer to any unbelief or any stumbling of the soul with regard to the promise: God's power. God is in the promise in his power. What he has promised he is also able to fulfil.

The second view of God in the promise given here is in the words, 'she judged him faithful.' Notice that this was not some emotional moment but a judgment. It was a clear exercise of the understanding. That is vital to faith. When the emotions become too involved with faith it is very apt to bring confusion into the mind. But where there is a clear understanding in the mind, faith is helped. In a very beautiful way, Sarah 'judged him faithful'. This was a judgment that she came to as she contemplated the promise. As she contemplated the power of God who had said to her, 'Is there anything too hard for the Lord?' she also contemplated his faithfulness. Faithfulness is another of the attributes of God. In other words, the glory of God with respect to these two attributes in particular was revealed to Sarah in connection with this promise, and she saw this. She saw that God was in the promise—that was clear to her.

And once she came to see that and to see the power of God and the faithfulness of God then she was able to close in with the promise—to believe it, and to believe that it would be fulfilled. She judged him faithful who had promised. God is faithful who also will do it. When he gives a promise, his power is behind it to effect its accomplishment, and his faithfulness is bound up with it. His power and also his faithfulness are behind it to secure that it should eventually take place. According to the time of year, according to the appointed time for the promise to be fulfilled, God's power and faithfulness would come into exercise. Sarah's faith embraced God in the promise, in his power and his faithfulness. And that's what she did, and that was the beauty of the exercise of faith in her heart.

Sarah received strength to conceive seed

When Sarah exercised faith in the promise we are told that she 'received strength to conceive seed'—something that she could not do before.

This was an exercise of faith. Because she believed the promise, strength was communicated to her so that although she was barren before, and now past the time of childbearing, yet she received strength from the power of God to conceive seed. Now, speaking for myself, I am not of the opinion that this refers to a miracle. Say for instance, if you take the virgin Mary, the seed being conceived in her case was a miracle, it was supernatural. A miracle was necessary because there was no human father involved. But here it is a receiving of strength, it was a communication by the power of God to this woman so that, where before she had not been in a condition to bear a child, she became able to bear one in virtue of the strength that she received. To my mind there is no doubt whatsoever about it, that through faith—that is, believing the promise, believing the power of God, believing the faithfulness of God—Sarah herself received strength to conceive seed. She was delivered of a child when she was past age because she judged him faithful who had promised. This wonderful—not miraculous—event took place. Strength was so communicated to her that the powers of nature, which had failed due to old age, were revived. The word here is 'strength'—they were strengthened. The powers of nature which had died in connection with her womb and her capacity to conceive seed were strengthened so that she became able to conceive seed.

This is attributed to the fact that she believed the promise. In the face of everything—in the face of the barrenness of her own womb, in the face of all that nature would say about how the promise could never be fulfilled, and unbelief saying amen to nature's objections—Sarah believed the promise of God and received strength to conceive seed. So that was a wonderful event. And from it arose also a very wonderful event. As it says here, 'Therefore sprang there even of one, and him as good as dead, as many as the stars of the sky in multitude, and the sand which is by the sea shore innumerable.' From this dead womb and from this dead man, there sprang an innumerable multitude. The Lord is able to do this!

Surely this is what the Lord does in a spiritual way also. The Lord's people very often feel how dead and barren they are in their soul—what darkness and death they feel, and how they lack the exercises of soul that they would desire to have. Yet this is what they are to look to, that the Lord is giving them a promise that he will strengthen them. And they are to receive that strength, and they are to receive an answer to the prayer, 'That in thee may thy people joy, / wilt thou not us revive?' (Psalm 85:6). Their faith must be in exercise because of the promise of God. Viewing his power, is he not able? Surely he brought the soul that was dead alive, and surely he has power to bring the soul that is alive to be revived! Surely that is clear! Surely even unbelief itself cannot find a hole in that argument! Surely God who brought the soul to be alive out of spiritual death ('you hath he quickened, who were dead in trespasses and sins') can revive that soul, which is alive but feeling its frailty and its failings and its darkness and its death and its backwardness and its coldness! Surely God can answer the prayer, 'That in thee may thy people joy, / wilt thou not us revive? / Show us thy mercy, Lord, to us / do thy salvation give.'

He is the one who says, 'I will help thee, I will strengthen thee.' These promises in the Word of God, with which the Word of God abounds, are fulfilled through the grace of faith in the souls of God's people. How wonderfully that is brought before us in Psalm 113! 'Thou didst me answer in the day / when I to thee did cry.' What next? 'And thou my fainting soul with strength / didst strengthen inwardly.' That cry was the cry of faith looking to the promise, and what happened was that the Lord fulfilled the promise. 'Though I in midst of trouble walk, / I light from thee shall have.' 'Surely that which concerneth me / the Lord will perfect make' (Psalm 138:7–8).

So it is that the grace of faith feeds on the promise, and the life of faith is strengthened and built up when it is exercised in connection with the promises. And in the case of Sarah, what tremendous fruit came of her faith, that 'there sprang of one, and him as good as dead, as many as the stars of the sky for multitude, or the sand which is by the sea shore innumerable.'

Sarah needed to plead the promise
I would just like to make one further point in connection with Sarah and her faith. The Lord had told her and Abraham that there would

be a time when this promise would be fulfilled. And the point that I want to make is that although Sarah knew that, that did not mean that she did not exercise the grace of faith. She did not say, in other words, 'Well, I know now that I'm going to have a child, the Lord has said so, he has given it to me in a promise, so now I can just forget about it.' The promise did not exclude her exercise of the grace of faith. And so it is with regard to all the promises given to all God's people. All the promises have a time when they are going to be fulfilled. But that does not mean to say that during the time until the promise is fulfilled they do not need to exercise faith, or plead the promise.

For instance, a particular time is referred to here when the promise is particularly precious—the time of a believer's death. 'These all died in faith.' When this time came, it was the time when the promise was to be fulfilled that the Saviour has given to his people, 'I go to prepare a place for you; and if I go to prepare a place for you I will come again, and receive you unto myself, that where I am there ye may be also.' That promise is to be fulfilled at death. And most people know that that promise is to be fulfilled at death. But they exercise faith in that promise all their lives, long before they die in the exercise of faith in that promise. That's what they rest in when they come to die, when they come to yield their spirits into the hands of the Saviour. They die in faith.

The preciousness of faith

Now of course the whole teaching of this chapter, as I have been endeavouring to emphasise, is to lay great stress on the preciousness of the grace of faith, and the preciousness of its proper living exercise as a means of strengthening and comforting and consoling God's people in this world. The more their faith is in exercise the more consolation and comfort they will have. They get strength and consolation and comfort from the promises.

Therefore let us seek grace to have the promise, to embrace Christ in the promise. The first exercise of faith is an embracing of Christ in the promise. It's not just embracing the promise, but embracing Christ in the promise, that is necessary. You take the promise of the gospel, which can be summed up in the words of Scripture, that 'whosoever believeth in him shall not perish, but have everlasting life'. That's the promise—'they shall not perish but have everlasting life.' In embracing this promise that the soul shall not perish but have everlasting life, faith embraces Christ in the promise. And those who embrace Christ in the promise have this hope and expectation that they shall never perish, but have everlasting life. None perish that him trust.

Here we are with Sarah later on in her Christian experience, and it's the same thing—she's not only embracing the promise but embracing God in the promise. You just look at the promises and examine them for yourself, these promises with which the Word of God is studded from Genesis to Revelation, and you'll see that to embrace the promise and the benefits that are held out in the promise cannot be done apart from embracing the God of the promise. And the God of the promise is God in Christ, so that you cannot embrace the promise without embracing the Lamb, the Saviour, the Mediator between God and man. May you and I learn to be living by such faith in this life.

May he bless his Word.

9 The grace of faith

HEBREWS 11:13

These all died in faith, not having received the promises, but having seen them afar off, and were persuaded of them, and embraced them, and confessed that they were strangers and *pilgrims on the earth.*

LORD'S DAY MORNING, 3RD OCTOBER 1999

IN the previous chapter the apostle has been stressing the great need of faith. In the concluding verse he says, 'But we are not of them who draw back unto perdition; but of them that believe to the saving of the soul.' Then he goes on to illustrate, by the inspiration of the Holy Ghost, the nature of faith and the fruits of faith, and the great cloud of witnesses in the Old Testament times. But both in Old Testament times and New Testament times these words are true, that the people of God live a life of faith. 'The life I now live,' said Paul, 'I live by the faith of the Son of God, who loved me and gave himself for me.' The people of God come up through the wilderness of time to the Jordan of death, to cross into the promised land, by faith leaning on their beloved, of whom their faith says, 'Thou, with thy counsel, while I live, / wilt me conduct and guide; / and to thy glory afterward / receive me to abide' (Psalm 73:24).

When we hear of the death of any of our neighbours or friends, those who are loaned to us in the world, we are reminded by that voice from heaven, that here have we no continuing city, and therefore we are exhorted to seek one which is to come. But when we hear of the death of one of the Lord's people, then we must remember that he or she died in faith—it was in the exercise of faith that they died. They died in faith. We are deeply conscious of the loss of the late Alasdair Gillies, who was here as an elder for so long, and who was so often seen by the congregation even after he went away to Dingwall, for his delight was to come back to communion seasons in the congregation in which he became a deacon and an elder. Now we hear that he died. That time came. But because it was the Lord's time, it was the proper time. We believe that something took place in heaven with regard to him, that the Saviour who loved him and gave himself for him, arose in his intercession at God's right hand, and with regard to him prayed or interceded for him, 'Father, I will that they also, whom thou hast given me, be with me where I am; that they may behold my glory.' Once that intercessory prayer rose before the throne of the majesty on high, then the sickle of death was sent to separate the soul from the body, and the soul was taken to be with Christ, which is far better. But we are told here that all the people of God—every one of them, no exception whatever—they all died in faith. Some might say, perhaps, that the case of Enoch was in some way an exception, because he was translated, body and soul. But we know that he walked with God and therefore was united by faith to Christ through the promise.

They all died in faith. And although we mourn their loss in this world, and it is proper for us to do so, they are happier now than they have ever been in time. They died in faith, but now they have laid aside faith, for faith was no longer needed. Now they see the king in his beauty in the land that is very far off. But we are left behind here and we should learn lessons from these events.

Now faith is what is especially brought before us in this chapter. And it is with regard to the grace of faith that we are particularly concerned this Sabbath morning

1. Now as you all know, or ought to know, faith is an exercise of soul, and faith as an exercise of soul has an object. And it is true that faith believes the Word of God, from Genesis to Revelation, believing

it to be the inerrant and infallible Word of God. Where that is not a conviction in the soul then there is no faith. Whatever people may say about having faith, without this they don't have it, and they will not die in faith if they do not believe the Word of God in its entirety. But the particular object of faith here and in the experience of God's people is the promise of God. They had faith in the promise of God. Therefore we shall consider that first of all—the object of faith is the promise of God.

2. Then secondly we shall consider the implanting of faith in the soul. Faith is the gift of God. Spiritual faith has no place in the heart of the natural man, because the natural man is spiritually dead. Therefore to believe what Arminians believe, that man is able to believe in his own power, that man is just spiritually sick, is a delusion. Multitudes are going to eternity believing that they are dying in faith, and with others believing that they are dying in faith, but they're going to eternity with a lie in their right hand. It is most important for us to remember and to seek to be taught by the Spirit of God as to how faith is implanted in the soul.

3. Then in the third place we shall consider the profession of faith. And we are told that profession of faith very clearly, that those who say such things declare plainly. They believe and speak—'I believed,' said David, 'and therefore I spake.' 'With the heart man believeth unto righteousness; and with the mouth confession is made unto salvation.' Those who die in faith, during their life they declare certain things to be true of them, and that is that they plainly seek a country. This is the beauty of a Christian profession, that everyone knows—even the ungodly—that they're not living for this world. They are strangers and pilgrims in this world, they are living for eternity, they are seeking a country which is not in this world—it is, as Paul says here, 'an heavenly country'. They are seeking, in other words, the eternal inheritance. That is seen clearly in their profession of faith in the world. You notice that it says 'plainly'. There's a great difference between people who are professing and you have doubt as to whether they really understand or they're really following Christ fully, through

good report and evil report. But here is something which we believe was illustrated in the case of our friend Alasdair Gillies, that he declared plainly—there was no question about it, he declared plainly by his profession of faith in Christ—that he was seeking another country. And that's where he is now, as to his soul.

1. The object of faith is the promise

We begin then by considering the object of faith, and that is the promise. Now, it was true of Abraham that he believed God—that is to say, he believed the promise. Now that raises a matter that requires some explanation. We read here that these 'died in faith, not having received the promises' (verse 13), and yet we are told that they did receive it (verse 17). So what are we to understand by the expression, 'not having received the promises'? We are to understand that the promise was not fulfilled in their day. But the object of faith is the promise, and Christ in the promise. In the first instance, it was Isaac in the promise, but Abraham was inwardly taught by the Spirit of God to look forward to the seed in whom all the nations of the earth would be blessed. And the Saviour tells us what the faith of Abraham saw in that promise—he saw the day of Christ. He saw the day of Christ and he was glad, he rejoiced in it. But Abraham's life in this world came to an end. He died in faith. His body was buried in Hebron and his soul went to be with Christ, which is far better. Yet he did not live to see the fulfilment of the promise. That was true of all the Old Testament saints (who are the 'all' particularly referred to here)—they did not see the promise being fulfilled but they believed it.

Now we are in a position of great advantage, dwelling in New Testament times, because the promise has been fulfilled. Christ has come, and Christ has died, and Christ has risen again, and Christ is now glorified in his holy humanity at God's right hand. We have the record of that. The inheritance of the better country that we look for, it's not a mere land of Canaan in this world. The Old Testament saints themselves were not satisfied with that. As a matter of fact, what did Abraham have of the land of promise when he came to die? Nothing but a grave—that's all he had of the land of promise in this world. But he had the eternal inheritance that the land of Canaan was intended to point to.

Now the Christ in the promise of God was the seed, of which Paul says, 'That seed was Christ,' in whom the nations of the world were to be blessed. It was the promise of the Messiah, the promise of the one who would bruise the head of the serpent, the one who would bring salvation into the world. This was the Shiloh of whom Jacob spoke, by the Spirit of prophecy (which is the testimony of Jesus), on his deathbed. When Jacob came to the tribe of Judah he said that the sceptre would not depart from Judah, nor a lawgiver from between his feet, until Shiloh would come. Judah was the tribe in which the Messiah would come, the one whom Abraham saw in the promise, and who Jacob saw in the promise, by the Spirit of prophecy—he saw Shiloh coming, the Prince of Peace. This view was given to Jacob, to David, to Barak, to Jephthae, and to all the others who are mentioned here, and others too—that Shiloh, the Prince of Peace, was to come, the Solomon of the New Testament, and that he was to come of the tribe of Judah.

But we are told more than that with regard to the Messiah. We are told that when he came of the tribe of Judah, he was to born in a certain place—Bethlehem. It was a small place in the eyes of the thousands of the tribe of Judah—but from there was to come forth from God him who was to be a governor who was from everlasting. So the one revealed in the promise, the Shiloh revealed in the promise, of the tribe of Judah, is a person who is from everlasting to everlasting, and that person is God. It is God who is the eternal being; it is God who is from everlasting to everlasting.

Then as the Scriptures were unfolded, we come to see that the everlasting God, who is to come from the tribe of Judah, is in the person of the Son. As you all know, there are three persons in the Godhead—the Father, the Son and the Holy Ghost. These are the same in substance—that is, they all possess the one divine nature, and as a consequence of that unity of the Godhead, they are not only the same in nature but they are equal in power and in glory. But they are distinguished by what we call their personal properties. They all possess the divine nature—the Son is everlasting, the Father is everlasting, the Holy Spirit is everlasting—but they are distinguished by their personal properties. It belongs to the Father, for instance, to beget the Son— that is, by a necessary and an eternal act. It is of course difficult if not impossible for us to think of an eternal act. When you and I think of an act we think of acts in time, things that take place in time, but here we are speaking about an eternal act, and that is beyond our comprehension. But it is an eternal act. And also—and we must emphasise this point—it is a necessary act. That is to say, it is not dependent on the Father's will. If it was dependent on the Father's will, the Son would be inferior to the Father, but he is not. The personal property of the Father is to beget the Son, and the personal property of the Son is to be begotten of the Father, and the personal property of the Holy Spirit is to proceed from the Father and from the Son.

The person who is from everlasting, born in Bethlehem-Judah, the Shiloh of the New Testament, is God the Son—God the eternal Son of the Father in truth and love. He was provided in the love of the Father to be the Prince of Peace. Why was that necessary? Why was such a prince needed—a prince that would be called the Shiloh, the Prince of Peace? Why would the Son of God be sent into the world and be born in Bethlehem-Judah? Why should there be a prince called the Prince of Peace? The reason is because sin entered into the world. Sin means that the whole human race is under the sentence of eternal death, and they have no peace with God, and they cannot ever, by any activities of their own, religious or otherwise, bring themselves to be at peace with God. It cannot be done, because that peace must include respect not only to the fact that God is an everlasting being but also that he is eternally and unchangeably holy and just.

God has said, 'The soul that sinneth, it shall die,' and therefore divine justice must be satisfied with any peace that is made. Any attempt to make peace between man and God must include divine justice being satisfied. And that shows you—it demonstrates clearly and unmistakeably—the impossibility of a sinful man or a sinful woman, like yourself and myself, ever making peace with God by any endeavours of our own to keep the law of God. The law of God is holy and spiritual and just and good, and we are carnal, sold under sin. And also to meet the claims that divine justice requires, the soul that sinneth shall die eternally. Therefore you see, as far as man is concerned, there can be no possibility of peace with God. All who depend on their own works to have peace with God will discover that to be true on the other side of death, when every delusion will be swept away. One moment in the eternal world, one moment before the throne of God, and every delusion and false hope will be swept away for all eternity.

But here is the true hope. Here is the hope of Israel and the Saviour thereof in the time of trouble—the Shiloh, the Prince of Peace. This was the blessing that Abel saw as he viewed the promise of God, that the seed of the woman would bruise the head of the serpent. This was the blessing that Abraham saw, this was the blessing that Isaac saw, this was the blessing that Jacob saw, as they viewed the promise of God. And this is what is now revealed in its fulness in the gospel of the grace of God, that God provided a Shiloh. God provided a prince—and what a prince! He provided David to rule over Israel, to guide them and govern them, and following David he provided Solomon, the prince of peace, with all the wisdom he had. The nation of Israel was raised to its most glorious state nationally at the time of Solomon's reign—although these were natural glories, yet they reflect some spirituality. But here in the New Testament we have the real prince. Now we can say, as he said himself, 'A greater than Solomon is here.' A greater than Solomon is in the promise. This prince is the Son of God, the king's Son—he is the Son of God.

And it was promised that he was to come forth from Bethlehem-Judah. In the Hebrew language, 'Bethlehem' means 'the house of bread'. It was there that the bread of life was born. It was there that the prince, the Son of God, came to possess a holy humanity. Although he was a prince who was the Son of God, he could not make peace with his Father just by being the Son of God. Something more was required—that divine justice would be satisfied. Here was the prince, the Son of God, the Son of the king eternal, immortal, invisible, the only wise God, and there was provided for him, in the womb of Mary, a holy humanity. In a womb in which man was never laid before, a virgin womb, by the power of the Holy Ghost, was conceived a holy humanity. And that holy humanity the prince of peace took into union with his divine person, and was born of her, without sin—holy, harmless and undefiled—Emmanuel, God with us, God in our nature. The Word, the personal Word of God, was made flesh, and dwelt among us, and we beheld his glory, the glory as of the only begotten of the Father, full of grace and truth.

The peace that this prince gives is a very wonderful peace. David brought peace to Israel by defeating the Philistines, by overthrowing all the enemies of Israel and bringing peace within the borders of the land, and Solomon maintained that peace. That princely peace was obtained and maintained by war, by human power, by human resource. But here is a prince, and this is a wonderful peace. It is a remarkable peace. It is a peace to be found nowhere else. It is peace through the blood of the cross! Not peace through divine power alone, not peace through the prince being the prince of peace alone, but peace through the blood of the cross of this prince. It is peace through the prince of peace who died the death divine justice required him to die, to atone for the sins of all his people, those who will die in faith. This is what he said to his disciples, 'Peace I leave with you.' 'I leave with you peace. Peace I leave with you in my will and testament. When I die I leave this in my will for you—peace.' 'My peace I give unto you—let not your heart be troubled, neither let it be afraid.' Here is what was in the promise—Christ, the prince of peace.

And something more—Christ is the prince of life. There is peace! Reconciliation to God for the soul! And there's life! Life that is hid in the prince of peace, life that is hid with Christ in God, life that is communicated to the soul! As the Saviour said, 'I am come that they might have life, and that they might have it more abundantly.' The life that they are to have is eternal life, it is an eternal inheritance. The

Saviour told them that when he died as the prince of peace, he was to rise again on the third day, and so he did. And what took place? He says, 'I go to prepare a place for you.' This is a very wonderful phrase, when you come to think of it. Surely heaven was prepared as the dwelling place of God from all eternity? And yet here is the prince of peace saying, as he is the prince of life, and as he rises from the dead by the power of an endless life and enters into heaven, 'I go to prepare a place for you. There are many mansions there, and I go to prepare a place for you.'

This brings before us that the prince of peace is also the high priest. As the high priest, Christ is not entered into the holy place made with hands, but into heaven, there to appear in the presence of God for us. That is the preparation for heaven. That is Christ preparing heaven for his people—he is there himself, and he is there in all the fulness and the merits of the peace that he obtained through the blood of the cross. You remember the high priest in the Old Testament— he took the blood, he put aside the veil, he went in before the throne of God, and he sprinkled the blood seven times on the throne. But when Christ went into the holy place not made with human hands, into heaven itself, and appeared before the everlasting Father, he was appearing before him as the prince of peace—he was presenting to him the atoning blood. Christ in the promise is bound up with the promise of the eternal inheritance. As we read later on, 'they seek a country'—a better country, a heavenly country—and that was procured for them by the prince of peace.

I was in Dingwall in 1935 and Rev. Malcolm Gillies was preaching on that text where it speaks of Christ not going to the holy places made with hands but into heaven itself. And he used this expression, an unforgettable expression: 'Christ went into heaven with all the merits of his finished work, and he said to the law and to the justice of God, "I claim this place for my people!" and they were silent, they agreed.' At one time the people of God in their spiritual experience felt that the law and the justice of God were against them, shutting them out from heaven, shutting them out from the favour of God, closing them in to eternal death. But now, when Christ appears in his glorified humanity before the throne of God, he said to them, 'I claim this place for my people!' and the law and justice of God agreed!

And then, Mr Gillies went on to say, 'The Holy Spirit comes into the soul, and the Holy Spirit says to the world and to the flesh and to the devil, "I claim this soul for Christ!"' Do you understand that? Do you feel pleasure in thinking about it? Do you feel a melting of soul in considering it? Well, we are coming to that now. This is how faith is brought into the soul. The Holy Spirit comes into the soul in the name of Christ and says, 'I claim this soul for Christ.'

2. The implanting of faith in the soul

That brings me now to how faith is wrought in the soul. As we read here with regard to Abraham, the beginning of faith being put in his soul was his call from Ur of the Chaldees. The beginning of grace in the soul is the call. 'O daughter, hearken and regard, / and do thine ear incline; / likewise forget thy father's house, / and people that are thine' (Psalm 45:10). The call is, 'Let the wicked forsake his way, and the unrighteous man his thoughts: and let him return unto the Lord, and he will have mercy upon him; and to our God, for he will abundantly pardon.'

Never forget, my dear fellow sinner, that faith comes into the soul when the Holy Spirit visits the soul with the effectual call. That's what's wrong with the religion of the present day. The faith that people are being taught today, I don't know what it is—it's not worth speaking about! The Word of God teaches that the faith that is the gift of God, is wrought in the heart by the Spirit of God in effectual calling. I've met people who came to this congregation from other churches, and they told me, 'We never heard the words "effectual calling" until we came to St Jude's.' If that is true, then they never heard about true faith. Let us be quite clear about it and understand these things. Faith is wrought in the heart in effectual calling.

Now when the Holy Spirit calls the soul, he calls the soul out of darkness. There was Abraham, and we are told by Stephen that the God of glory appeared to Abraham in Ur of the Chaldees—that is to say, when he was in the darkness of idolatry. When he was in the darkness of idolatry, the God of glory appeared to him in the command to leave his father's house and the people that were his, to go forth to a land that the Lord would show him. Now surely when that happened, when he felt the authority of the Word of God in that command, then Abraham realised that he was in darkness, realised that he was in the land of idolatry, realised that he was a sinner in the sight of God and had been sinning against God all the time that he dwelt in Ur of the Chaldees.

And so it is, that when the Holy Spirit comes, through the Word of God, to take a sinner out of the kingdom of darkness, the first thing he does is convince him that he is in the kingdom of darkness, because as men and women are by nature they do not think about that. The idea of being in the kingdom of darkness is completely foreign to them. They may hear it from the pulpit but they don't believe it in their souls. They never felt it in their souls. But when, by the light of the Word of God, the Holy Spirit begins to work, he brings the sinner to know that he is in the kingdom of darkness, that he is ignorant of God, and ignorant of sin, and yet he gives him a sense that his sins and his iniquities are coming between him and God, and he finds himself in darkness. There's a disposition or an inclination in that soul now. Because he has felt the authority of God's Word in convincing him of sin, he now feels the authority of God's Word with regard to the promise.

That is what the Shorter Catechism means when it says that effectual calling includes enlightening the mind in the knowledge of Christ. The Holy Spirit enlightens the mind in the knowledge of Christ in the promise. Let's come over to the New Testament. We hear there, 'God so loved the world, that he gave his only begotten Son, that whosoever believeth in him should not perish, but have everlasting life.' Here's the promise—Christ in the promise, and by the work of the Holy Spirit the soul is enlightened in the knowledge of Christ in the promise. As I've said already, Christ is the Prince of Peace, the peace which comes through the blood of the cross, and

115

when the Holy Spirit takes of the things of Christ and reveals them to the soul, the soul gets a view of Christ in the promise of the gospel, and whosoever believeth in him shall not perish, but have everlasting life.

Now in the words before us we have a very beautiful piece of instruction given to us with regard to the activity of soul when faith comes into exercise. First of all, they are in the condition of not having received the promises, but having seen them afar off. Of course that applies in a particular way to the Old Testament. But it also applies, in a certain way, to the sinner under the New Testament. The sinner convinced of sin sees the promise as afar off. Do you know about that? Do you know what it means to sit here as a sinner in the sight of God? Christ in the promise is brought before you, and you're told that whosoever believeth in him shall not perish, but have everlasting life. But Christ in the promise is far off! You cannot lay hold of him! Do you know what that means? Do you know what it means, to break your heart that you cannot lay hold of Christ in the promise?

How do they come then to lay hold of Christ? Listen to this carefully, step by step. Don't be carried away with mere emotion. First the sinner hears about Christ in the promise, but cannot lay hold of the promise—it's far off. Now here is the next thing: 'They were persuaded of them.' They believed that the promises were true. Where faith is in living exercise, where the soul coming to the exercise of laying hold of Christ in the promise by the hand of faith, that soul is persuaded that the promise is the promise of God, and that it is true, that whosoever believeth in Christ shall not perish but have everlasting life. They are persuaded of it.

And here is the next thing. As you remember, in the definition of effectual calling in the Shorter Catechism, we read of the Holy Spirit persuading and enabling—persuading them first, and then enabling them. Well, here is the enabling—'They embraced them.' They embraced the promise, they embraced Christ in the promise. They are persuaded this is the promise of God. 'How wonderful it is that I, a sinner, if I believe in Christ, will not perish, though I deserve to perish!

God would be just if I perished forever, but I shall not perish, but have everlasting life. I am persuaded that this is true.' And now there is an embracing of Christ in the promise. The soul is now enabled to embrace Christ in the promise, and so he is united to Christ for time and for eternity, he has peace with God through the Lord Jesus Christ, and is an heir of everlasting inheritance. He shall never perish. 'And no man', said the Saviour, 'is able to pluck them out of my hand.'

3. The profession of faith
So there you have faith in the soul. They begin to live now by faith. And living by faith they have a profession.

Now you must be careful, as you're dealing with solemn matters, spiritual matters, matters on which you need the light of the Word of God. You cannot divorce these two things that God has joined together—belief in the heart with the confession of the mouth.

Very well, here is the profession. They confessed (or professed, if you like, and it's a better word, perhaps) that they were strangers and pilgrims on the earth. They were strangers and pilgrims on the earth. Do you remember, when you came to Christ, how you felt a difference between yourself and the world? Perhaps, when you went into the office and met the others with whom you worked and with whom you were quite friendly, you felt a stranger? Or when you went into the ward and met the other nurses, you felt different? You were no longer one of them. You were a stranger on the earth. You were no longer of the world, though you were in it. And they knew that too. Perhaps when you were going along the road they crossed over to the other side in case they would meet you, some who were your friends in former days. They acknowledged that you were different from what you were. All this was demonstrating a profession—that you were a stranger in the world, and also that you were a pilgrim. This world was not your rest. The Old Testament believers desired a country, but they desired a better country, a heavenly country. And that was their profession of faith. Their faces were set Zion-ward. 'So they from strength unwearied go / still forward unto strength, / until in Zion

117

they appear / before the Lord at length' (Psalm 84:7). And when do they appear in Zion before the Lord at length? When they die in faith.

'They that say such things' profess them, they declare something. There's a declaration in the profession that this is a people who desire a better country. They receive the good in the providence of God, but that does not satisfy them. They have a spiritual mind. They have faith, faith that is looking to be fed from the Word of God, faith that is looking for the soul to be prepared for eternity. They are pilgrims in this world.

'Therefore God is not ashamed to be called their God.' Many a time they are ashamed of the weakness of their profession themselves, but God knows and Christ knows their profession. See what he said about Abraham—he called him 'my friend'. How was Abraham his friend? He was his friend of course in believing the promise and being reconciled to him, but he was his friend in this way, that while his camp moved through the land of Canaan, he kept the way of the Lord. There were the Perizzites, the Hivites and all the Canaanitish tribes, all worshipping their own gods, and here was this man, this solitary tent of the family, being instructed in the way of the Lord to keep the way of the Lord, and God knew that. He said, 'I know Abraham. In the midst of all the darkness of the land of Canaan and all the idolatries of the tribes that are there, I know this man, that he will instruct his family to keep the way of the Lord.' And so in the midst of Canaan he was the friend of God. All the Canaanitish tribes were the enemies of God, because they were idolaters, but Abraham was the friend of God.

Or look again at another apparently dark period in the history of the church. When Christ died, when his body was on the cross, there were two men, and perhaps you'd say to begin with that their profession was not all it should be, although they did not go in with the judgment when Jesus was sentenced to death—Nicodemus and Joseph of Arimathaea. But when the time came, their profession was made clear. They went in and they got the body of Jesus, took him down from the cross and laid him in the tomb of Joseph of Arimathaea—

they laid him in the tomb where no man was ever laid before. What a wonderful thing the gospel is! How sad that the people of our day do not even hear about it! Nicodemus and Joseph of Arimathaea now became the friends of Christ in an outstanding way. We would have been ready to conclude, well, their profession was weak—but you see, in that dark hour, when it came to the testing time, it all came out then, that they were the friends of Christ. When his body was without a spirit, when he was dead, they were the friends of Christ who took care of his body. Christ left that body in their hands to be laid in the grave until he would rise on the third day.

So it is true of all the people of God. He is not ashamed to be called their God. And so they come to the better country, to the city that God has prepared for them, the dwelling place that God has prepared for them, the rest that remaineth to the people of God. And they reach that place when they die in faith. Then they receive the promise in its fulness, the promise to be with Christ, which is far better—absent from the body and present with the Lord. They die in faith—that is, united to Christ, body and soul. Not only do they die believing that their soul will be with Christ, but they die in faith that the body that they leave behind they will meet again. The body they leave behind will be raised on the resurrection morning. God is not the God of the dead. The God of Abraham, Isaac and Jacob; the God who is not ashamed to call Abraham and Isaac and Jacob his people— he is not ashamed of their profession—he is the God not of the dead but of the living. That's what the Saviour said, pointing to the resurrection. On the morning of the resurrection, when time shall be no longer, they will be united together—the body will be raised as a glorified, incorruptible body to meet the glorified soul.

Then Abraham and Isaac and Jacob will be there. Many souls will be there, and many souls united to bodies that we knew in this world. They died in faith. The spirits of just men are made perfect, but there is something they are still waiting for—for the body to be raised. As surely as Christ's body was raised from the dead, although it was incorruptible, so their corruptible bodies that saw corruption will be raised on the morning of the resurrection to be united with their glorified spirits, and then they will be brought to God's right hand— not just one soul here and one soul there, but the whole multitude, like the stars of the sky for multitude. 'They shall be brought with gladness great, / and mirth on ev'ry side, / into the palace of the King, / and there they shall abide' (Psalm 45:15).

Now what about yourself? What about yourself? Have you this hope, that if death came to you, you would be one of those of whom we read here, 'they died in faith'?

May he bless his Word.

10 Faith in the promises

Hebrews 11:13–16

These all died in faith, not having received the promises, but having seen them afar off, and were persuaded of them, and embraced them, and confessed that they were strangers and pilgrims on the earth. For they that say such things declare plainly that they seek a country. And truly, if they had been mindful of that country from whence they came out, they might have had opportunity to have returned. But now they desire a better country, that is, an heavenly: wherefore God is not ashamed to be called their God: for he hath prepared for them a city.

Wednesday, 14ᵀᴴ March 1984

WE have been considering in this chapter the various instances which bring before us the grace of faith and the exercise of that grace in the souls of the people of God, who live a life of faith upon the Son of God. This is what distinguishes them from the world that lies in the wicked one, that they live a life of faith upon the Son of God. In doing so they can say with the apostle, 'He loved me and gave himself for me.' They may have many doubts about that latter point due to unbelief and temptations of one kind or another, but the fact remains—and the Scripture declares it plainly—that those who are living a life of faith upon the Son of God are loved by Christ and Christ gave himself for them. And the faith that they exercise is of course the gift of God. It is something that was not in them as they are by nature, but it was wrought in the effectual call of the Holy Spirit.

These all died in faith, not having received the promises

At this point in the chapter the apostle says that 'these all died in faith'. They not only lived a life of faith upon the Son of God, but when they came to die, they died in the exercise of faith. That will be true of all the people of God in this world. As surely as they live a life of faith upon the Son of God, so they die in faith.

Faith finds its object and its exercise with regard to the promise of God. The apostle points out in this verse that there are two things in connection with the promise of God. One is the promise itself; the other thing is that which was promised, or in other words, what the promise contains. These two things arise in connection with all God's promises. There is the fact that he has promised and that he will fulfil whatever he promises, and there is also what the promise contains. The Old Testament saints all died in faith, not having received the promises—that is to say, not having received what was in the promise, not having received the fulfilment of the promise.

All the promises of God are yea and amen in Christ Jesus, and the particular promise which is referred to here, and on which the faith of God's people in the Old Testament was exercised, was the promise of the Messiah—the promise of the seed of Abraham. As Paul points out in his epistle to the Galatians, that seed was Christ. The Old Testament saints exercised faith in the promises, although the promise of Christ coming was not yet fulfilled in their day. But although the substance of the promise had not yet been fulfilled, that did not prevent them from believing in the promises, as we see here. That's the first point that arises here. With regard to the sum and substance of these promises, which was the coming of the Saviour, they had not received the fulfilment of these promises when they died. Yet they died in faith believing that Christ would come. That's what we read in connection with Abraham, and the Saviour told the Jews that 'Abraham saw my day, and he rejoiced'. He was glad when he saw by faith the day of Christ. And where did he see it? He saw it principally in the promise that in the fulness of the times, in his seed would all the nations of the earth be blessed—that as surely as Isaac was born into the world, so in the fulness of the times the New Testament Isaac would come into the world also.

The Old Testament saints and the promises
Now the great value of these verses is that they not only draw that distinction between the substance of the promise and the promise itself, but they also set out for us how faith exercises itself in the promise. And that should be of great value to us if we are concerned as to whether or not we have believed in the promise, as to whether or not we've got the grace of faith which is the gift of God.

With regard to the substance of the promise, the first thing mentioned here is that they saw it afar off. They saw it afar off with respect to time. When Abraham saw Christ's day, he saw it as a day that was far off in time—he saw the coming of Christ into the world as something afar off, something that was to be fulfilled in God's time.

The next thing about the promise that is mentioned here is that they were persuaded of it. They were persuaded that what was in the promise was true and would be fulfilled. With respect to the coming of the Messiah whom they needed for the salvation of their souls, for deliverance of all their sins, they believed that he would come—they were persuaded of it. They were clear on it. When they thought of the substance of the promise, although it was far off with respect to time, yet they were persuaded of it. There was a confidence of mind with regard to the substance of the promise, that however long it would be, the promise would be accomplished and fulfilled.

So there is a discerning of the substance of the promise, there is a persuasion of the certainty of the promise being fulfilled, and now there is this last point—there is an embracing of the promise. Faith is a warm embracing of the promise. In the case of Abraham and the other Old Testament saints, as they viewed Christ in the promise, and that he was the Messiah and the appointed Saviour who was to come in God's great name to save, they were persuaded that he would come and work out salvation, and they warmly embraced the promise and leaned on it for time and for eternity.

The New Testament saints and the promises

Now when we come to our own day, to New Testament times, faith still has the same exercise, although it is not an exercise in the promise of one who was to come—it is the exercise of faith in connection with one who has come.

The particular promise that Abraham and the Old Testament saints believed (as they declared by their life) was that they sought a country, and we are told it was a heavenly country. Their faith went out to Christ in the expectation of being in heaven with him.

When the gospel comes to a sinner and is blessed by the Holy Spirit, and the sinner comes to feel his sins and his iniquities and feel his need of salvation, heaven does indeed appear very far off then. But he is confronted with the gospel, which is just the promise elaborated, set out in a greater fulness than it ever was to Abraham, Isaac and Jacob, or Noah, or Sarah and so on. The gospel is set before us by the Messiah who did come, who wrought out redemption for his folk, who poured out his soul unto death, and in whom there is eternal salvation for the very chief of sinners. And the promise is that whosoever believeth in him should not perish, but have everlasting life. That is the promise of salvation and the promise of heaven, for God so loved the world, that he gave his only begotten Son, that whosoever believeth in him should not perish, but have everlasting life.

Now the soul coming to the exercise of faith first of all discerns the substance of the promise—that is, Christ and his salvation. They get spiritual understanding and light on the Saviour as the Son of God in our nature, and on the salvation that he wrought out in his sufferings unto death, and they see that Christ has wrought out salvation. Just as in the Old Testament they saw it far off in the future, so in New Testament times the exercise of faith takes to do with something that is far off in the opposite direction, something that took place two thousand years ago—something that took place on the tree of Calvary where Christ finished the work that the Father gave him to do, and wrought out a complete and free and full salvation for a number that no man can number. The soul in the exercise of faith sees and discerns Christ in his person and in his work.

And he is persuaded of it. He is persuaded that Christ is a Saviour able to save to the very uttermost all those who come unto God by him. He is persuaded that this is God's Saviour, that this is God's salvation. He has a confidence of mind about this, his mind is settled on this point, that Christ is the Saviour able to save to the very uttermost.

Therefore the soul comes to believe in Christ, and that is what is meant by 'embracing'—embracing Christ in the promise of the gospel. That is the exercise of faith. The soul sees the substance (the Saviour, Christ, in the promise and in the everlasting gospel), and is persuaded that whosoever believeth in him shall not perish but have everlasting life, and as a sinner with no good thing in himself or herself but altogether unworthy, and they embrace Christ in the everlasting gospel. And in embracing him they have the hope of salvation, they have the hope that they will never perish, they have the hope of eternal life.

There follows from that exercise of faith that they are justified by faith, they have peace with God, and the moment the soul is united to Christ that soul is saved in the Lord with an everlasting salvation. Now, as a fruit of this exercise of faith, what flows forth from this spiritual exercise of faith are the graces of the Spirit. We must ever remember that all the graces that we speak of, like faith and love and hope and repentance and so on—they are all exercises of soul, but the soul is not divided into different compartments. The soul is a spirit, and it has the simplicity of that which is spirit. In the same way we speak about the faculties of soul, but we don't mean that the conscience is there and the understanding is there and the will is there and the affections somewhere else, as though there were different compartments in the soul. The understanding is the soul knowing, the will is the soul choosing, the affections are the soul loving or hating, and the conscience is the soul passing judgment. So with regard to the graces of the spirit. These are all exercises of soul, and it is beautifully described here by the Holy Spirit through Paul: 'Having seen them …

being persuaded of them … and embraced them.' You should seek to lay hold of these three things in connection with the spiritual exercise of soul—having seen them, being persuaded of them and embracing them.

Strangers and pilgrims on the earth

Now flowing from their faith comes this—they made a confession. The heart believes unto righteousness, with the mouth confession is made unto salvation. Wherever there is faith, saving faith, of the nature I have been endeavouring to describe, there will be a confession.

We are told what the confession was. 'They confessed that they were strangers and pilgrims on the earth.' They confessed this—it flowed forth in their life, walk and conversation—that this was not their home. This world is not their home. They are strangers here. They are pilgrims here. They are strangers in the sense that they are not at home in the world; they are pilgrims in the sense that they are journeying on to their home. So it is true of the people of God, that they are strangers in this world. As Christ himself said, though they are in the world they are not of it. They are not at home in the world, or in the company of the world. They are pilgrims journeying Zion-ward. 'They that say such things declare plainly that they seek a country.'

They desire a better country

'And truly, if they had been mindful of that country from whence they came out, they might have had opportunity to have returned.' Abraham could have returned to Ur of the Chaldees, and so he could have had the opportunity to return had he sought it, but he did not. He turned his back on it. He was finished with it, he was done with it. So it is a mark of the people of God that they are finished with the world; they do not go back to the world. They do not weary of Christ, they do not weary of separation from the world, they do not go back to the world. 'So henceforth we will not go back, / nor turn from thee at all. / O do thou quicken us and we / upon thy name will call'

(Psalm 80:18). They do not go back but they desire a better country, that is, a heavenly one.

That brings me back to this point, that the end of their earthly journey is in death. They all died in faith. They died believing that they were going to the better country. That means that they believed that there was a better country, that there was an afterlife, that there was a heaven, and also a hell. When they died in faith, they hoped and believed that they were going to the better country. That's what they were seeking. They believed that when they were leaving this world, as to their souls they would go to a better country. And they also believed that when they left their bodies behind, it was only for a time. Their bodies had to be left behind at death, and had to go down into the grave's devouring mouth and see corruption. But they died in faith in the resurrection, that the body that they left behind would yet arise on the morning of the resurrection and be reunited with their soul, to be with Christ after the resurrection in the better country. They died in faith of the resurrection.

God is not ashamed to be called their God

'Wherefore God is not ashamed to be called their God.' They are often ashamed of themselves, but what a wonderful thing it is for this to be said, that God is not ashamed of them. He is not ashamed to be called the God of those who live a life of faith on the Son of God, who have eschewed all appearance of evil, who have left the world and its ways and all that belongs to it, and are on their journey Zion-ward. God is not ashamed to be called their God. That is a great wonder to them, but it is a fact. The Scripture says it here. 'God is not ashamed to be called their God.'

He has demonstrated that he is not ashamed to be called their God, because he is to have them with him forever. 'He hath prepared for them a city.' God has prepared a place for them—a city, a house of many mansions, as it is variously described. The sum and substance of it is a place prepared by God where they are to be with him, and with him in everlasting glory, as we were singing in Psalm 73: 'Thou with thy counsel, while I live, / wilt me conduct and guide; / and to thy glory afterward / receive me to abide' (Psalm 73:24). That is faith, and that is a dying in faith, for God has demonstrated that he is not ashamed to be called their God.

He does not say, after they've been in the world and following on for a time, 'Now they've done this and that and the other thing, and now I'm ashamed of them and I'll leave them.' No! But he says he has prepared for them a city, a city that has foundations, whose builder and whose maker is God. Heaven is a place in the universe of God which God has prepared, where his glory shines forth with an effulgence and a glory that can be seen nowhere else.

This is the place concerning which Christ said, 'In my Father's house are many mansions; if it were not so, I would have told you. I go to prepare a place for you.' It's prepared by the Father and by the Son, and the Lord's people are prepared by the Holy Spirit to be in it, through getting the grace of faith in this world and through following Christ through good and evil report. Being sanctified perfectly at death, they are 'brought with gladness great / and mirth on every side, / into the palace of the king, / and there they shall abide'.

We too need this faith

This is what you and I should be seeking above everything else in this world—that we too would have this precious faith, this precious gift—that in this world we would be living a life of faith on the Son of God—that it would be evident in our walk and life and conversation that we are strangers and pilgrims in the world, that this is not our rest, and that we are seeking the rest that remaineth to the people of God.

God's people are often ashamed of themselves—often! They are often ashamed of themselves and often cast down. They feel like this in view of all the privileges that they enjoy, and all the fulness that is to be found in Christ. But God is not ashamed of them. None perish that him trust. They shall never be put to shame, world without end. God is not ashamed of them—he has accepted them in the beloved, and they are his children, journeying on Zion-ward, to be at last in the place where the glory of God shines. You see, wonderful though it may be to think of it, they will not be strangers and pilgrims any more when they enter heaven. They will be at rest.

And no wonder that they should be at rest, when you think of it! When you think of the glory of God shining in heaven, and you think of the throne of God and the glory of God filling heaven, then perhaps you think, 'I wonder, really, if I would be at rest?' Well, you will be, and I'll tell you why. Because the glory shines in the face of the Lamb in the midst of the throne, and the one whom they see when they enter the palace of the king is the king himself, the Lamb. The glory of God shining in the face of Jesus Christ throughout endless ages is the inheritance that God will give them, which excels in beauty. They will be at home. And of course they will be at home with the people of God, and that is throughout endless ages.

Therefore let each one of us seek with our whole heart and mind that we may be united to Christ by faith, and let us be seeking from the Scriptures to learn more and more about faith and its exercises. You see, that is very strengthening, is it not? I am sure now that you are here, and you may say to yourself, and perhaps you say it very often, 'Well, my faith is very weak, sometimes I can hardly see it.' But be honest with yourself. Must you not say that you have been persuaded of the promise? And must you not say that you have embraced the promise?—that this is your only hope for eternity?—Christ in the everlasting gospel—that you are resting in him for time and for eternity? Well, that is faith, saving faith, as the apostle brings before us here.

May he bless his Word.

11 The journey of faith

HEBREWS 11:14

For they that say such things declare plainly that they seek a country. And truly, if they had been mindful of that country from whence they came out, they might have had opportunity to have returned. But now they desire a better country, that is, an heavenly: wherefore God is not ashamed to be called their God: for he hath prepared for them a city.

LORD'S DAY MORNING, 7TH OCTOBER 1990

IN this chapter we have an account given of examples of those in whose heart the Holy Spirit wrought the grace of faith. Faith is not to be found in the heart of man as he is by nature, for we are told that 'that which is born of the flesh is flesh; and that which is born of the spirit is spirit' (John 3:6). All that is in the heart of unconverted, graceless men and women is the flesh, and that which is born of the flesh. Therefore no member of the human family has the grace of faith without that gift being wrought in their hearts by the Holy Spirit.

Now we read in the Word of God that 'with the heart man believeth unto righteousness' (Romans 10:10). That is to say, the grace of faith is hidden in the human heart. It cannot be discerned by those who have no knowledge of what is in that heart, for no man knoweth the things of a man, save the spirit of man which is in him. Therefore no one can know for a certainty about the grace of faith being in the soul of another person, except in this one way: 'With the heart man believeth unto righteousness; and with the mouth confession is made unto salvation.' So all who have the grace of faith also have a confession. These two things cannot be separated. It is impossible for there to be the grace of faith in the heart without the outward confession or profession being made in that person's life and conduct.

Therefore we read here that those who died in faith had a confession or a profession that they were strangers and pilgrims on the earth (verse 13). And just as faith has a language—'I believed, and therefore have I spoken'—so it is true that the profession of faith, where it is genuine and sincere, has a language. We are told this here, 'For they that say such things declare plainly.' They make a declaration. Their life and conversation has a voice as surely the grace of faith in their heart has voice also.

We read here of those who died in faith. It is evident that there came a time in their life when for the first time they exercised that grace of faith in which they died. We are told that they were strangers and pilgrims on the earth. They began a certain journey and they died in faith. The journey which they began was the journey beginning the life of faith. Paul speaks of this life: 'The life which I now live, I live by the faith of the Son of God, who loved me, and gave himself for me' (Galatians 2:20). With regard to the patriarchs, we are told here that 'truly, if they had been mindful of that country from whence they came out, they might have had opportunity to have returned.' This journey that they began, which came to an end at death when they died in faith, was a journey from another country. In the case of Abraham there was a natural journey from Ur of the Chaldees—that is the natural country that he left. But from the spiritual point of view the country that he left was the land of darkness, the land of idolatry. He left that land because he began to live a life of faith.

1. First of all we shall consider that those who are referred to here have left the land of darkness, the land of idolatry, and have begun the journey of faith.

2. Secondly we shall consider their particular exercise of faith so that we may examine ourselves as to whether or not we have begun this spiritual journey. Abraham left Ur of the Chaldees to journey to

the land of Canaan, but as far as the life of faith is concerned he left the land of darkness and idolatry because he saw the promise.

3. And then we shall notice how they were known in their life and walk and conversation. They were known in this twofold way: firstly that they were strangers, and secondly that they were pilgrims. The life of faith is the life of a pilgrim. 'They were strangers and pilgrims on the earth', and this fact had a voice, it gave a testimony, a profession. This fact was declaring something with regard to them— that they are seeking a country. They left the one behind and they are seeking another, because of the desire they have, and because the other country is a better country. It is not better merely because there's a better climate or because they have better opportunities to acquire riches or power or honour—it is a better country because it is a heavenly country.

4. Lastly we shall notice what is declared with regard to the God who is their God. 'God is not ashamed to be called their God.' He does not consider it a matter in which he is humbling himself when he is called their God, but rather it is something he delights in. This is manifested in a certain way—'he hath prepared for them a city'. He is to abide with them—this is to be their heaven and the heaven that they are to share with him. When John had a view of the Bride, the wife of the Lamb of God, carried to the great city, the holy Jerusalem descending from the hands of God, it was a place where he saw no temple, 'for the Lord God Almighty and the Lamb are the temple of it. And the city had no need of the sun, neither of the moon, to shine in it: for the glory of God did lighten it, and the Lamb is the light thereof' (Revelation 21:22–23). 'He hath prepared for them a city.'

1. Beginning the journey of faith

Now let us firstly consider the beginning of their spiritual pilgrimage. It is true of every one who comes to have the grace of faith in the world that they have a beginning to that pilgrimage. When they began that pilgrimage they were found in the land of spiritual darkness, in the land of ignorance of God, as Abraham was in Ur of the Chaldees, in the land of idolatry, serving diverse lusts and pleasures. We have reason to believe from his name that Abram (as he then was) was a high priest in the land of idolatry, dwelling in darkness and ignorance of God, dwelling in the shadow of death, a sinner in the sight of God. Therefore we read with regard to all those who began this pilgrimage, 'He out of darkness did them bring, / and from death's shade them take; / these bands, wherewith they had been bound, / asunder quite he brake' (Psalm 107:14). These were bands that Abraham could not break. They are bands that you, who have the grace of faith, could not break. They are bands that no human power can break. They are bands that parental love and authority and affection cannot break. They are bands that the preaching of the gospel itself alone cannot break. 'These bands wherewith they had been bound'—they were bound in the land of darkness, bound under the shadow of death by the power and the reign of sin.

What broke these bands in the experience of Abraham? There he was in Ur of the Chaldees and he didn't have a thought about eternity, he didn't have a thought about his soul, or about his sins and his iniquities. We see that what broke in upon him was the word of God coming with commanding power, 'Get thee out of thy country, from thy kindred, from thy father's house' (Genesis 12:1). It was a call—the call of God to Abraham to forsake the foolish and live, to come out of the land of darkness. 'Let the wicked forsake his way, and the unrighteous man his thoughts: and let him return unto the Lord, and he will have mercy upon him; and to our God, for he will abundantly pardon' (Isaiah 55:7).

We are told by Stephen that the word of God made a certain impression on the soul of Abraham (Acts 7:2–4). The God of glory spoke to our father Abraham. This word of God became the word of the glorious God. The word of the God of glory was shining into the darkness of Abraham's soul, bringing into the darkness of his soul the fact that there was a God, that he was a God of glory, and that all the dumb idols which he served were mere vanities. Behind that call was this view of the God of glory, the God of infinite power, the God of justice, the God of holiness, the God to whom sin is an abomination, the God who has said that the wages of sin is death.

All those who have begun this spiritual pilgrimage were brought out of darkness by the Word of God convincing them that God was— that God is the glorious being that he is, that he is one who cannot be turned aside, he is one that the soul cannot forget, but he is one whose word has authority and whose word is a word of power. Where there is the word of a king there is a word of power (Ecclesiastes 8:4), but when it is the word of the king immortal, invisible, the only wise God, then it is a word of power indeed. The sinner, hearing the Word of God calling him from his sins, finds himself in darkness, finds himself in the shadow of death. Just as surely as when Lazarus heard the voice of Christ in the grave and was awakened, he found himself in darkness, he found himself in the grave—so the sinner finds himself in his sins. This is a realisation that he never had before, coming home in his spiritual experience, that God is, and that he is sinner in the sight of God, and that he is under the shadow of death and ready to perish unless he is delivered from his sins.

The same voice that called to Abraham to go out of this country directed him to follow the word of God 'into a land that I will show thee'. Now the same thing is true with regard to this spiritual pilgrimage, that the soul is given a mind to follow the Word of God, not only in forsaking his sins but by returning to God. 'Let the wicked forsake his way, and the unrighteous man his thoughts: and let him return unto the Lord, and to our God, for he will have mercy upon him.' God shows the soul the way to return. God was to show Abraham the way to the land of Canaan, yes, but he also showed him the way to return to God, the way to come to peace with God, the way to obtain the pardon of sin. And God showed him what? Well, Christ tells us what Abraham saw: 'Abraham saw my day, and was glad' (John 8:56). He saw a day! Instead of darkness, the light of the day! Instead of darkness, the light of the day of salvation! 'This is the day which the Lord hath made; we will rejoice and be glad in it' (Psalm 118:24). Abraham saw that day, the day of Christ, the day which brought light into his soul. The day of Christ is the day of the gospel of Christ. The Lord showed him that there was a way of return to God, that there was one who said, 'I am the way, the truth, and the life: no man cometh unto the Father, but by me,' the one who consecrated the new and the living way through the rent veil of his flesh for a soul to return to God. This is the object of faith—Christ, his body broken, his blood shed.

You remember when the Saviour died outside the city of Jerusalem, a certain event took place inside the temple. When that great cry ascended from the cross of Calvary, 'It is finished', the veil of the temple was rent in twain from the top to the bottom to show that the way into the holiest of all was now manifest. Christ died and paid the ransom price for the sins of his people. Here is the way. Through Christ and him crucified, through the broken body and the shed blood of Christ, through the rent veil of Christ, through Christ in the everlasting gospel, faith enters in. That is the beginning of the journey— when faith enters in by Christ; when faith says, viewing Christ in the gospel, 'This is the gate of God, the gate provided by God.' 'This is the gate of God, / by it the just shall enter in. / Thee will I praise, for thou me heard'st / and hast my safety been' (Psalm 118:20–21). 'In dwellings of the righteous / is heard the melody / of joy and health' (Psalm 118:15). When faith embraces Christ, the sinner is saved in him with an everlasting salvation, and the sinner now comes to rejoice in God's salvation, to see Christ's day and to be glad. That's the beginning of the life of faith.

There is no other way to begin the life of faith, apart from effectual calling. I've often mentioned the fact to you, because it needs to be stressed, that a kind of witless, worthless religion is going about under the name of evangelical Christianity, which disregards effectual calling altogether. You must be quite clear in your mind: there is no such thing as faith in the soul of any sinner without effectual calling, without being brought out of darkness into God's marvellous light.

2. Faith is exercised about the promise
Let us notice now in more detail the beginning of this life of faith in its first exercise. The first exercise of faith is to look to the promise.

They 'see the promise afar off'. Where did Abraham see Christ's day? Where did he see it? Did he see it in a vision? No, he did not! He saw it in the promise, 'in thy seed shall all the nations of the earth be blessed'. 'And to thy seed,' Paul says,—not 'to thy seeds', but 'thy seed', singular, which is Christ (Galatians 3:16). So Abraham saw the day of Christ in the promise. And those who now live under the New Testament dispensation see the day of Christ in the promise of the gospel.

Now, there is a difference between the way that faith was exercised in Christ in the promise, in the case of Abraham, Isaac and Jacob and all the fathers, and the way that a soul in our day sees the promise. What is the difference? The difference is that Abraham saw Christ in the promise as the seed, the one that was to come. But when faith is exercised now in the New Testament dispensation, with the revelation of God's Word complete, we now see the day of Christ as the day that has come. The day of Christ has passed. We see the day of Christ with these words written over it, 'It is finished.' We see the day of Christ as something that has taken place, of which we have the record before us—his birth into the world, his magnifying the law, his satisfying divine justice, his dying and rising again to sit at God's right hand. Faith looking to Christ in the promise now, looks to Christ as the one in whom there is eternal salvation, and looks to Christ as the one who has said with regard to his salvation, 'Whosoever believeth in me shall not perish but have everlasting life.' But the promise of the day of Christ is a day that, as far as we are concerned, has finished long ago. 'Having seen them afar off.'

And there is another sense in which Christ in the gospel is 'afar off' to the soul in the New Testament dispensation. Yes, the gospel is brought nigh to them, but it is something they cannot embrace in their natural strength. Whatever sermons they hear about Christ, about his person, about his work, about his love, about his grace, the promise seems to them afar off because of their inability in their own strength to receive Christ in the promise. That they all learned; that they all have to learn—that faith is the gift of God. It is not spun out of a person's soul.

Now we notice now how this takes place. How does it take place, that the promise becomes so near that they embrace it? Well, we are told that they 'were persuaded of them'. That is how the promise is brought near, so near that it was embraced—they were persuaded of it. They were persuaded of various things with regard to Christ in the promise. They were persuaded that Christ was the Son of God, they were persuaded that the salvation that was in Christ was a salvation altogether suitable for sinners such as they had discovered themselves to be. They were persuaded of that. They reached a firm conclusion about this, that Jesus Christ was the Son of God, that he was the appointed Saviour, that he had finished the work that the Father gave him to do. They were persuaded that the promise was true, that 'whosoever believeth in him should not perish, but have everlasting life' (John 3:16). Whosoever! They came to see that that 'whosoever' included themselves. You see, part of the distance between them and Christ in the promise was their own unbelief. They were putting themselves outside the 'whosoever'. They were saying to themselves, 'I need more conviction of sin, I need more of this, I need more of that, I need more of the next thing.' When they would get that, then they were going to come with it and say to Christ, 'Now here I've got more conviction of sin, I've got more sense of sin, and now grant me thy salvation.' Well, it does not happen like that. That's unbelief—coming with a price in your hand. Whatever it may be, however small it may be, whatever its nature may be, you shut yourself out from the promise by your unbelief. But now they were persuaded of this: 'Whosoever believeth in him shall not perish, but have everlasting life.' They were persuaded of that.

And now what happened? Well, we are told here, they embraced the promise. Now the word 'embrace' here implies and includes giving a welcome. When people meet one another they embrace. When somebody comes to your house and you embrace them, you're giving them a welcome. That's what this means here. This embracing means the soul giving a welcome to Christ in the promise—embracing him, giving him a welcome, saying to Christ, 'Come in!' As Christ himself says, 'Behold, I stand at the door, and knock: if any man hear my voice, and open the door' and give me a welcome, 'I will come in to him, and will sup with him, and he with me.' The welcome is their embracing of Christ in the promise. That's the beginning of this life of faith. When they embrace him, it is a warm embrace. It's not just a mere exercise of intellect, it's an exercise of heart—it is a heart embracing of Christ in the promise of the gospel.

3. They are strangers and pilgrims

That's the beginning of this journey. And immediately there follows the confession. 'With the heart man believeth unto righteousness', in the secrecy of his or her soul. But there's also an outward confession, 'with the mouth confession is made unto salvation' (Romans 10:10). That confession is that they are 'strangers and pilgrims in the earth'. In thinking of them as strangers, the view brought before us is that they don't belong to this world any more in the spirit of their minds. Strangers not conformed to this world, but they are transformed, by the renewing of their mind (Romans 12:2). When Ruth said to Naomi, 'Thy people shall be my people' (Ruth 1:6), it was goodbye to the young men and women of Moab. She was done with them. They were strangers to her, though they were her kindred, and though that was her native land. 'They are in the world,' said Christ with regard to these people, 'but they are not of it' (John 17:11, 16). Just like their glorious head. What did he say with regard to the world? 'I was a stranger, and ye took me not in.' (Matthew 25:43). The people who had faith, *they* took him in. Oh yes, *they* embraced him. Mary and Martha and Lazarus in Bethany, they had an open door in their home for Christ because they had an open door in their hearts for Christ.

They are strangers. And also they are pilgrims. As strangers, they are showing they are not of this world. As pilgrims on the earth, they are seeking another country. I just remark in passing that the Pope has recently said that the churches should come together, and he uses this phrase, 'No longer strangers, but pilgrims.' But the Word of God says that the people of God are strangers *and* pilgrims. So he perverts this part of the Word of God, saying that we should be pilgrims but not strangers, by which he means not strangers to one another. You see the subtlety of that? These poor creatures in all these churches in ACTS, the new council, Action of Churches Together in Scotland— they are swallowing the idea that they're pilgrims going to heaven, according to their idea, in friendship with one another. But who said the Pope was going to heaven? The Pope is going to purgatory, according to Roman Catholic dogma. Is that where Church of Scotland ministers are going? Is that where bishops of the Church of England are going? Is that where Methodists and Baptists are going? What a farce! However, we have neither part nor lot with them. We are speaking about the people of God just now, not those who are just wearing a cloak of a profession that's worthless.

The people of God are pilgrims in the earth. They are journeying somewhere else. They are just passing through the world. This is not their rest. It is polluted, and a polluted rest will not do for this people who are hungering and thirsting after righteousness. Their separation from the world, their desires, their longings, and their attitudes all make it quite plain that they are not living in the world for the world— they are in the world but they are not of it, because they are just passing through it.

'They that say such things declare plainly that they seek a country.' When Abraham, Isaac and Jacob were going about in tents, that wasn't their rest. They were seeking a country. The Lord's people in this world, those who are living a life of faith upon the Son of God, they are not seeking their rest in this world, they are on their way to another land. That's where their desire is. Their desire is in a better country, a heavenly country. This world cannot satisfy the Lord's people because they are spiritually-minded, because they have spiritual thirst, because they have spiritual hunger, because they need spiritual satisfaction. The things of this world cannot meet their case. Their desire is to a heavenly country.

We also read here another thing with regard to them, and that is this: 'If they had been mindful of that country from whence they came out, they might have had opportunity to have returned.' They might have had opportunity to return to the country from which they came out—to the darkness of the world, to the amusements of the world, to the companions of the world, to the honours of the world, to the riches of the world—they might have gone back there to that country from whence they came. But this desire in their souls is something that finds nothing in that country. They seek a heavenly country. They seek a better country. The late Charlotte MacKay, a godly woman in Thurso, used to say, 'I like to follow my desire.' That was a favourite phrase of hers. If she had a desire to go to a communion, she used to go, however difficult it was for her. And I have no doubt whatsoever that her ultimate desire was to be with Christ, which is far better, and that she followed that desire at last into Emmanuel's land. No doubt that was true of others also. It is true of our friend who last Friday reached the better country, Mrs MacPherson from Kames, whom we knew over these many years. She was a stranger and a pilgrim in the world. She made it plain, very plain, that her desire was not in the things of time but the things of the gospel, the unsearchable riches of Christ. And her desire was to the better country, the heavenly country.

4. God is not ashamed to be called their God

Something is prepared for every one of the desires of God's people. He opens his hand wide and meets the desire of everything that lives (Psalm 104:28). 'He will accomplish the desire / of those his name that fear' (Psalm 145:19). He has his own provision for all these desires. And he has his provision for the desire for a better country. God has prepared for them a city. There is a time when the life of faith is to come to an end, when the life of wandering and being a pilgrim is to come to an end. God has also made provision for their desire that they would be with Christ, and with Christ in the city which hath foundations, whose builder and maker is God, where God has his everlasting habitation, where God dwells with men and where there is the Lamb in the midst of the throne and his people gathered round the throne. 'He hath prepared for them a city.'

'In my Father's house', said the Saviour, 'are many mansions: if it were not so, I would have told you. I go to prepare a place for you. And if I go and prepare a place for you, I will come again, and receive you unto myself; that where I am, there ye may be also' (John 14:2–3). Then there will be an end of wandering. It will all come to an end in the rest that remaineth for the people of God—an end to the waves that went up and down, an end to the many troughs they were in, an end to the storms and the difficulties and the trials and the temptations. They are all now come to an absolute and final end in the stability of eternal glory in the city that hath foundations, whose builder and whose maker is God. At this time we have been hearing of the passing of Mrs MacPherson, whom we knew in this presbytery, and recently one on the Isle of Lewis, and many more. When they came to the end of the journey, 'they died in faith'. Many a time they had been worried about faith and they had many a question about their faith, but they all died in faith, and faith in the promise. What promise? Christ's promise to each one of them: 'I go to prepare a place for you.' What a wonderful place! Prepared by the Father. Prepared by the love of the Father and the love of the Son.

'And if I go and prepare a place for you, I will come again, and receive you unto myself.' What does that mean? Well it means this, my dear friend, that the soul that gave a warm welcome to Christ in the gospel and embraced him in the promise in this world—that soul dies in faith, and on the other side of death Christ gives that soul a warm welcome into heaven. 'Come in!' 'Well done, good and faithful servant, enter into the joy of thy lord, joy that shall never end!' What a warm welcome Christ gives to the souls of his people as they are carried by the angels into everlasting glory! There's a warm welcome waiting for them at the end of this journey.

And there is this to it also, that 'God is not ashamed to be called their God'. By the grace of God, they were not ashamed to be on God's side in this world, and now God is not ashamed of them. They will be openly acknowledged before the great white throne, and they will be openly acknowledged in the sense that he has built a city, where he and his people may dwell together. They will dwell together with the angels and the archangels and the cherubim and the seraphim in the glorious city that has foundations. The light of the glory of that city is the glory of God. This city has no need of the sun to shine in it, for the glory of God lightens it, and the Lamb is the light thereof.

God and his people will dwell together in everlasting love, ever-lasting communion and everlasting joy, world without end. And how small the troubles and the trials they have in this world will appear when they think of that, when they will taste of that! As Paul said, these troubles and trials and temptations only worked for him a great and exceeding weight of glory. One moment in glory, and all their sufferings will be remembered no more.

'These died in faith.' They reached the end of their journey. The journey they began in faith is the journey that they ended in faith. They ended it embracing the promise, embracing Christ in the promise, 'I will come again, and receive you unto myself.' And as they received him by faith, so he will receive them in the arms of eternal love on the other side of death.

Now here is the question for you and for me, when we hear of one of the Lord's people being taken away. They died in faith and they are now, as to their souls, with Christ, which is far better. Are you and I in that pilgrim band? Are you and I companions to those who are strangers in the world? Or are we of the earth, earthy? Are we following the world and its ways and its pleasures and its kingdom, all of which will come to nothing? When death will come we shall have to go to the eternal world. Will we be of those who will be welcomed by Christ on the other side of death?

May he bless his Word.

12 The city God has prepared

HEBREWS 11:14–16

For they that say such things declare plainly that they seek a country. And truly, if they had been mindful of that country from whence they came out, they might have had opportunity to have returned. But now they desire a better country, that is, an heavenly: wherefore God is not ashamed to be called their God: for he hath prepared for them a city.

LORD'S DAY MORNING, 7TH JANUARY 2001

IN this portion of the Word of God we have set before us a great cloud of witnesses of the Old Testament church. And it was true of them, as surely as it is equally true of the great cloud of witnesses in the New Testament church, that they lived a life of faith upon the Son of God. As the apostle Paul said, 'The life which I now live in the flesh I live by the faith of the Son of God, who loved me, and gave himself for me.' That was also true of the cloud of witnesses under the Old Testament dispensation. And when they came to an end of their days in this world, they all died in faith. They all died as believers in the Lord and Saviour Jesus Christ. And because they so died in him, when their souls left their bodies, their souls went to be with Christ, which is far better, in the city which is referred to here and described by the Saviour, 'In my Father's house are many mansions: if it were not so, I would have told you. I go to prepare a place for you. And if I go and prepare a place for you, I will come again, and receive you unto myself; that where I am, there ye may be also' (John 14:2, 3).

Yesterday John Angus MacLeod, who was a professing man and an elder in this congregation for many years, having reached the age of 92, came to the end of the journey, and this morning the wife of Mr Iain MacKinnon the elder [Isobel MacKinnon] came to the end of the journey also. But the end of the journey was arrival at a city. It was not an end except with regard to this world—it was a journey over the Jordan of death into the promised land, the heaven of God's people, a state of glory to which they must all come. That's where they will all come when Christ's time comes to appear before his Father with the great cloud of incense of his intercessory prayer and plead, 'Father, I will that those whom thou hast given me'—given me in the everlasting covenant, and given me by creating faith in their souls to believe in me—'may be with me where I am, that they may behold my glory, the glory that I had with thee before the world was.'

1. Now, in considering these words, we shall consider first of all the faith of Abraham. He has been described, and properly so, as the father of the faithful.

2. Secondly we shall consider that which follows faith in the heart—that is, the profession of faith. These two things the Word of God joins together, for 'with the heart man believeth unto righteousness, and with the mouth confession is made unto salvation' (Romans 10:10). As David says, 'I believed, therefore have I spoken' (Psalm 16:10). Abraham believed, Isaac believed, the people of God believe in every age and generation, and 'they that say such things declare plainly that they seek a country'. They have a profession that they are in the world but they are not of the world, that this world is not an abiding city for them, for here they have no continuing city, but they seek one which is to come.

3. And surely it will be fulfilled, that as they seek it, so the time will come when they shall find it. And therefore we shall consider, in the last place, what God has prepared for the end of the journey. It is a city—not a land, but a city, 'a city that hath foundations, whose builder and whose maker is God'.

1. The faith of Abraham

Let us begin first of all then with considering the faith of Abraham. Abraham's faith illustrates the faith of the people of God in every age and generation; a faith which stands not in the wisdom of men but in the power of God.

When we look at the faith of Abraham we discover that it is bound up with a call. 'By faith Abraham, when he was called to go out into a place which he should after receive for an inheritance, obeyed; and he went out, not knowing whither he went' (Hebrews 11:8). A call came to Abraham, in the midst of idolatry, in the darkness of paganism, in the darkness of spiritual ignorance, in the darkness that is in the human mind as we all come into the world, ignorant of the God of eternity. Abraham, then named Abram, as he worshipped in Ur of the Chaldees was engaged in the worship of idolatry, not the worship of the true God. In other words, Abraham, when he was called, was a sinner engaged in a life of sin, engaged in a false religion, engaged in having a false hope with regard to the issue of his soul passing into the eternal world.

So it is at the present day. There never will be the grace of faith, the faith that Abraham had, without a call. Not a call from one land to go out to see another land, but an effectual call coming to the sinner in his sins, coming to the sinner pursuing his sins, coming to the sinner as it did to Saul of Tarsus on his way to Damascus, when his heart was filled with hatred against Christ and his people, and in that very sin he was called. This is true of all the people of God and always will be, today, and in every age and in every generation. It will be true of all those in whose heart the Holy Spirit works the grace of faith: it will be done in connection with a call.

Stephen tells us in his address to the Jews (Acts 7:2–56) that the God of glory appeared to our father Abraham in Ur of the Chaldees. He would have been quite content there, adding sin to sin, treasuring up wrath against the day of wrath. But the God of glory appeared to Abraham there. A ray of the glory of God shone into his soul. It shone into his soul through the word of God. When the word of God came to him, calling him to leave Ur of the Chaldees, he turned his back on his sins. It was the same call in other words which was addressed to sinners on another occasion and is still addressed to us now through the gospel, 'Let the wicked forsake his way, and the unrighteous man his thoughts: and let him return unto the Lord, and he will have mercy upon him; and to our God, for he will abundantly pardon' (Isaiah 55:7). This ray of the light of the glory of God gave Abraham to see his danger in Ur of the Chaldees—his danger in sinning against God, his danger in being ignorant of God, his need of a salvation that he could not provide himself, and that he could not find in the worship of idols in Ur of the Chaldees.

So when that call came, it came as a word of power. A ray of divine light, a ray of divine glory entered the darkness of the soul of Abraham, and Abraham believed then that God was. As we read earlier on in the chapter (verse 6), 'He that cometh to God must believe that he is.' The light that began to shine in the darkness of Abraham's understanding gave him to know that God—the God whose voice was addressing him and calling him to forsake the foolish and live—was the real God, the God who is not a dumb idol like the blinded nations fear, but the God who could speak, and he realised that this God was speaking to him. This God was calling on him to forsake the darkness of Ur of the Chaldees and to turn his face from it. One of the effects of this call was not only to give Abraham to know that he was a sinner, that he needed salvation and needed to be delivered from the wrath to come, but it also gave him a desire to follow the light of this world, to follow the word of God. And therefore we read that he went out. Although he did not know where he was going, one thing he did know, and that is that he would follow the light of the word of God.

As he followed the light of the word which God gave him, God revealed to him something else. He revealed to him a promise. In that promise there was revealed to him a seed—a seed in whom all the nations of the earth would be blessed. The Lord Jesus Christ, speaking about Abraham's experience, says, 'Abraham saw my day, and was glad' (John 8:56). Abraham saw that day in the promise of the word of God with regard to the seed who would be of such a kind that in him—in that seed—all the nations of the earth would be blessed. That being so, then it must have been obvious to Abraham that that seed could not be a mere man. As Paul tells us, 'that seed was Christ' (Galatians 3:16). If all the nations of the earth were to be blessed in him then it could not be a mere man, especially if they were to be blessed with God's blessing. With God's blessing, then, Abraham understood in the light of the promise given to him that in the fulness of the times there was to come one who would be a Saviour, a Saviour in whom all the nations of the earth would be blessed—that is, in union to whom all the nations of the earth would be blessed.

I am of the mind that at a later stage Abraham got a little more light on the seed. There came a time in his experience that he had a son, whose name was Isaac. And the word of God came to him—the same word that brought him out of Ur of the Chaldees, and the same gracious, irresistible power with that word—telling him to proceed to a mountain in the land of Moriah to offer up his son Isaac, 'thine only son, whom thou lovest' (Genesis 22:2). You remember, when they made the journey, and left the servants behind at the bottom of Mount Moriah, and the father and the son together ascended the mount, that Isaac asked a question. 'Here is the fire and here is the wood: but where is the lamb for a burnt offering?' (Genesis 22:7). The lamb was Isaac, Abraham's only son, whom he loved. We cannot but think that as Abraham went through that experience, which was a trial of his faith and his love, the Lord so shone into his soul that he understood that the seed was a divine person—and not only that he was a divine person but that he was the only begotten and well-beloved Son of the everlasting Father. So in the promise of the seed, 'Abraham saw my day,' said Christ. 'He saw my day, and was glad'—he rejoiced with joy unspeakable and full of glory because he saw the day of Christ. He saw that the Saviour was to come in the fulness of the times, just as Isaac himself came and was born to him in the fulness of the times—and that he would be a lamb for the burnt offering, as Isaac prefigured, and who would be thereby the Saviour of the lost and the undone.

Now Abraham also knew that all nations of the earth would be blessed *in Christ.* 'Men shall be blessed in him.' 'In' there means 'in union to him', being united to him.

Abraham believed God. He believed the promise—he did not receive the fulfilment of it, but he received the promise itself. Just in the same way, he received the promise of a son, Isaac, but the fulfilment of the promise did not come till the appointed time. He understood, in the measure of light which he had, that Christ was to come, and he believed in him and trusted in him, and was united to him by this faith wrought in his heart by the Holy Ghost. He was united to Christ in the promise. He died in faith, not having received the fulfilment of the promise, but he received the promise itself, which is to say, he received Christ in the promise. And to this very day, and right down through the New Testament dispensation until time shall be no longer, those who are effectually called are enlightened by the Holy Ghost through the gospel with regard to the promise of Christ, and are united to him. The promise is, 'God so loved the world, that he gave his only begotten Son, that whosoever believeth in him'—whosoever therefore is united to him—'should not perish, but have everlasting life' (John 3:16). It is true of the soul of Abraham and the souls of believers in our day and generation, that when they were effectually called, faith was wrought in the heart to believe *in Christ* in the promise of the Word of God, that 'whosoever believeth in him should not perish, but have everlasting life'. That is the faith that is of the operation of God, not the faith that stands in the wisdom of men, but the inward grace and teaching of the Holy Spirit enlightening the mind in the knowledge of Christ in the promise.

Abraham believed in a promise which was to be fulfilled, but you and I, if we are believers, believe in a promise that has been fulfilled—that the true light is now shining, the darkness has passed, Christ has come. Christ has glorified the Father on the earth and finished the work which the Father gave him to do. Now Christ is held out in the Word of God, and sinners are called on to believe in the Lord Jesus Christ and so they shall be saved. And so thou shalt be saved.

148

So the faith of Abraham is still the faith of the people of God—they have faith in Christ in the promise and thereby they are united to him, and thereby receive the forgiveness of sins, and thereby come into the favour of God, and thereby have the life that shall never end.

2. Abraham's profession of faith

The next thing that we are to consider is the profession of Abraham. Now Abraham was living in, and came out of, Ur of the Chaldees, a land of idolaters. And when he came to the Promised Land it was full of idolaters—Hivites, Hittites and all the tribes of Canaan—all idolaters. And so the people of God, when they are united to Christ, they come out of the world, but they are still in the world. They are still moving up and down in the world, as Abraham moved up and down in the land of Canaan among these Canaanitish tribes. 'He sojourned in the land of promise, as in a strange country, dwelling in tabernacles with Isaac and Jacob, the heirs with him of the same promise' (Hebrews 11:9).

Now as they were in the land of Canaan, moving up and down together in the land of Canaan, they were 'strangers and pilgrims on the earth' (verse 13). Canaan was not their rest. It was a type of the rest, but it was not the rest. And neither is this world the rest of the people of God. They are here and they are strangers. They are in a strange land, surrounded by the world, surrounded by those who are dead in trespasses and sins, those who are despisers of Christ, those who are living according to the course of the world. Abraham and Isaac and Jacob, as they dwelt in their tabernacles with their families, were moving about among these Canaanitish tribes—they had their own flocks, they had their own tabernacles, they had their own families, but they were strangers in that land. That was not their rest. They were journeying through that land, they were strangers, they were pilgrims. They were looking past the land of Canaan and they were looking for a city—'a city that hath foundations, whose builder and maker is God' (verse 10).

If you want to make a distinction between the two words, 'builder' and 'maker', by 'maker' we understand God planning the city, and by 'building' we understand him forming the city. Heaven is a place that God has planned, where there is to be a manifestation of his divine glory, and where those who lived a life of faith in this world are to have their eventual rest.

As to his profession in this land of Canaan, in the world, in the midst of this idolatry, we are told that God knew Abraham. He knew Abraham in this way—that Abraham would instruct his family to keep the way of the Lord. In the tabernacle of Abraham, in the house of Abraham, was the church of God. And in the house of Abraham was the way of the Lord. The manifestation of God's way of salvation was made known to Abraham, and Abraham was teaching his family the worship of God, the glory of God. So as Abraham, Isaac, and Jacob were in their tabernacles, travelling through the land of Canaan in the darkness of heathendom, their profession was that there was light in their dwellings. Just as surely as in the darkness of Egypt there was light in the dwellings of the children of Israel, so in the tabernacles of Abraham, Isaac and Jacob, there was spiritual light.

God knew that Abraham would teach his family the way of the Lord, to keep the way of the Lord, the worship of God, the revelation that God had given to Abraham in the promise. Abraham was a witness to the fact that there was another God. The gods of the Hivites and the Hittites and the rest of the Canaanitish tribes were 'idols dumb, which blinded nations fear' (Psalm 96:5). But the God of Abraham, Isaac and Jacob was the God 'by whom the heavens created were' (Psalm 96:5)—he was the God who had spoken to them, and by faith in his word they became strangers and pilgrims in the world, who kept the way of the Lord.

The profession of all who have faith is the same now—they keep the way of the Lord. They worship God according to his mind, for as the Saviour said, 'they that worship God must worship him in spirit and in truth' (John 4:24). They are 'of the circumcision, which worship God in the spirit, and rejoice in Christ Jesus, and have no confidence in the flesh' (Philippians 3:3). Their worship is a testimony against idolatry. In our day and generation people are trying to make idolatry and Christianity one worship. These people show they are on their way to hell. They may be called bishops and archbishops, and they may get big obituary notices in the papers, but they are not on the same journey as Abraham, Isaac and Jacob, or the people of God in our day and generation. The people of God testify to the pure worship of God and they keep the way of the Lord. They keep the Sabbath day holy, too. These idolaters, like the Canaanitish heathen, break the Sabbath day. They go to the supermarket, they go to the football match. The Saviour says, 'if any man love me, let him keep my commandments' (John 15:10). Let him keep my commandments, and my Father and I will come and abide with him, through the grace of the Holy Ghost (John 14:23).

And as well as a profession with regard to the way of the Lord and the worship of God, they have a profession with regard to the way of salvation. There is none other name under heaven given among men, whereby we must be saved, but the name Jesus (Acts 4:12). Abraham saw Christ in the promise, and you (if you are one of the people of God) also got a view by faith of Christ and him crucified, the Lamb of God that took away the sin of the world.

The people of God are witnesses because they walk in the way of God's commandments. And they are strangers. They are walking against the world—they are in the world but they are not of it, just as Abraham was in the land of Canaan but he was not of it. Abraham knew that this land was given to him by promise, because it was the land in which the seed was eventually to be born, but as far as he was concerned, the only place he would have in that land was a grave in Hebron. That's where his dust lies this very day. Abraham and Sarah, Jacob and Leah, and Isaac and Rebecca are buried in Hebron—that's all they had in the land of Canaan. And that's all that the people of God will have in the world at the end of life's journey—a place where their dust is to remain until the morning of the resurrection. The Muslims have built a mosque over the grave of Abraham, Isaac and Jacob, but that mosque will not prevent their bodies rising on the morning of the resurrection, and neither will anything prevent it for any of the people of God, wherever their dust lies. When the resurrection morning comes, that body will rise from the dead to be united to the soul that at death passed into everlasting glory.

3. The place that God has prepared for them

So this is the end of the journey. And that's the last point—the place that God has prepared for them.

There is no more journeying. No more journeying, not another step! Once their souls go into the city that hath foundations, whose builder and maker is God, it's an end of travelling, it's an end of being pilgrims, it's an end of being strangers. They will be at home. There will be no idolaters, no Sabbath breakers, no rejecters of Christ. All who will be gathered there—the angels, the archangels, the cherubim and the seraphim, the spirits of just men made perfect—they will all glory in Christ and they will all have come to an eternal Sabbath. 'There remaineth a rest to the people of God' (Hebrews 4:9). A rest—it's an end of the journey. The city is an end of the journey, and it is 'a city which hath foundations'—it will never be moved, world without end. This is their dwelling place for ever and ever and ever, with Christ the Lamb in the midst of the throne, and the Father in him, and the Holy Ghost by him, and Christ leading them to fountains of living waters and feeding them on the glory of God shining in the person of Christ.

This is the place where they are to come, because they die in faith. They die united to Christ, and therefore their souls being united to Christ depart immediately, and are immediately made perfect in holiness, and are with Christ, which is far better. Of course it is sad for those who are left behind. Look at the mourning there was when Stephen died—that eminent man of God—and the mourning when Jacob died. It's sad for those who are left behind, when we see the people of God taken away and their places becoming empty in the church below. But we must remember that for them it is far better. For them the day of their death is better than the day of their birth because they die in faith. Their souls are united to Christ, and in the twinkling of an eye they are with him, made perfect in holiness, seeing the king in his beauty in the land that appeared very far off at one time, but they are now in the city that hath foundations, whose builder and maker is God. The journey has come to an end. They reached the 'sabbatismos'—the rest that remaineth to the people of God, an eternal Sabbath to the people of God. There's an eternity of worshipping Christ, an eternity of worshipping God in Christ, an eternity of viewing the glory of God in Christ, an eternity of everlasting blessedness in the city that hath foundations, whose builder and maker is God.

There are words that Christ spoke to his disciples that we ought to remember. He told them that his journey in this world was coming to an end and that he was to leave them. When he told them that, they were sorrowful, they were sad. But he said to them, 'If ye loved me, ye would rejoice, because I said, I go unto the Father: for my Father is greater than I' (John 14:28). You and I, we must watch our spirits and be careful when the people of God are taken away not to be overcome with overmuch sorrow. We must remember that though we loved them, we may rejoice that they have reached the city, they are now at rest, they are now with Christ, which is far better. I remember being very much impressed with that during the time in 1956 when I was in Rhodesia. Rev. James Fraser was labouring there, and he and I were very friendly. We were the same age. He was quite keen that I would stay in Rhodesia with him, but I did not see that that was my duty at the time. But I do remember this, that when he died, I could not grudge. Although I was sorry, I could not grudge. He had laboured so hard, he was worn out, as he was 'the man who loved the people'. That was the name the Matabeles had for James Fraser, 'the man who loved the people'.

We should be exercised by remembering also that the body, being still united to Christ, remains in the grave till the morning of the resurrection. Abraham knew that. He made these arrangements with the son of Heth when Sarah died, so that he would have one place in the land of Canaan where the dust of Sarah would be, and his own dust, and the dust of Jacob and Leah (Rachel died, you remember, on the way down). He knew that they would be there, still united to

Christ, until the morning of the resurrection, when time shall be no longer, and when this world is to go back into the nothingness from whence it came. When Christ receives his people, he will raise their bodies from the grave's devouring mouth, and raise them like unto his own glorious body, so that they are the many sons, bearing the image of Christ on their souls—yes, and on their bodies—the many sons brought to glory. So, as I was saying recently [in another sermon], not only is the bride of Christ clothed in a glorious garment but she is all glorious within.

Now the last point to make is this: 'If they had been mindful of that country from whence they came out, they might have had opportunity to have returned.' But they did not return. They followed on to know the Lord, whose going forth is as the morning (Hosea 6:3). The first rays from the sun of righteousness (Malachi 4:2) that shone in their souls gave them the first view that they had of Christ by faith. That sun is now risen to its meridian height. The sun shall no more go down when the soul goes into everlasting glory.

They did not go back. They followed the Lamb through good and through evil report. You remember the hundred and forty-four thousand on Mount Zion that we read of (Revelation 14:3). They were singing a song that no one could sing but those who were redeemed from the earth. What else was said about them? Not only that they sang that song, but that they 'followed the Lamb whithersoever he went' until they reached that place where the Lamb is. They did not go back. They might have had opportunity to have returned. But now they desire a better country. They see that there is a better country, and they have a desire towards that better country, and 'he will accomplish the desire / of those that do him fear' (Psalm 145:19).

'Wherefore God is not ashamed to be called their God: for he hath prepared for them a city.' 'This God is our God,' said David, 'for ever and ever: he will be our guide even unto death' (Psalm 48:14). He will guide us even unto death and over death into everlasting glory. Just as the children of Israel came to the Jordan, and the Jordan opened and they passed over into the Promised Land, so it is true with regard to the people of God. The city is prepared for them and they are prepared for the city—they are clothed in the righteousness of Christ, and in their souls they have the work of the Spirit, regeneration and sanctification, completed at the moment of death. So they now have the image of the Son in the faculties of their souls and in the members of their bodies, and in their glorified persons they are saved in the Lord with an everlasting salvation.

And in this city they have a song, and it's a song to the Lamb in the midst of the throne. They can never forget that the Lamb who is now in the glory of the midst of the throne was once in the darkness and pain and sorrow of the cross of Calvary, numbered with the transgressors in order that they might be saved through the shedding of his precious blood. So their praise is to the Lamb who loved us and gave himself for us, and washed us from our sins in his own blood. To him be glory and dominion, world without end.

May he bless his Word.

13 Abraham

HEBREWS 11:17–19

By faith Abraham, when he was tried, offered up Isaac: and he that had received the promises offered up his only begotten son, of whom it was said, That in Isaac shall thy seed be called: accounting that God was able to raise him up, even from the dead; from whence also he received him in a figure.

WEDNESDAY, 21ˢᵀ MARCH 1984

WE were endeavouring to consider on the last occasion the faith of Sarah, and in these words we have brought before us a particular exercise of faith on the part of her husband Abraham. Sarah and Abraham were heirs together of the promise of life. They were both united by faith to the Messiah who was to come, they were both born again, both followers of the God of Israel. And when we come to this particular case of Abraham, the father of the faithful, then we can expect that his case would very likely be an eminent one. Although all the people of God have the same grace, there some are more prominent in one grace than another. Abraham was very prominent in the grace of faith, and Peter was strong in the grace of courage and attachment to the Lord Jesus Christ, for example.

Now it is very often the case when the people of God are prominent in a certain grace, that that is the very grace which God tries. That happened with Peter, as we know. Because he did not follow the Lord closely, and because he was rash in thinking that his natural courage would do in the place of following the Saviour and looking to him alone, when he was tried that very grace of courage failed.

Let us turn to Abraham, who was prominent in the grace of faith. We are told that he was tried. He had many trials of one description and another but on this occasion he was tried in an outstanding way. We read that 'God did tempt Abraham' (Genesis 22:1). Of course we are told in the Scriptures that God does not tempt any man—that is to say, God does not tempt any man to do evil. But the meaning of 'tempt' in this connection is that he was tested, or he was tried. This teaches us that it is common to faith to be tried, that the grace of faith is a grace which is often tried. It belongs to the experience of those who have the grace of faith that they do have trials, in order that their faith might be seen clearly in its exercise. God did not need to see that—he knew that Abraham had the grace of faith. But it was brought out in the exercise of this particular trial. And so it will ever be in the history of the people of God, that each one in his or her own way will be tried in connection with the grace of faith. And it is through the grace of faith that they obtain the victory and come out on the other side of the trial.

The trial of Abraham's obedience

Now this trial of Abraham's had in it many elements. It was in connection with God's command. The command was, 'Take now thy son, thine only son Isaac, whom thou lovest, and get thee into the land of Moriah; and offer him there for a burnt offering upon one of the mountains which I will tell thee of' (Genesis 22:2). The Scriptures tell us here that Abraham offered up Isaac. So the first thing with regard to the exercise of faith is that it is obedient. It is called 'the obedience of faith'. Wherever faith is, it is in the nature of faith to be obedient to the Word of God. That was demonstrated here in the case of Abraham in an outstanding way.

The trial of Abraham's natural affection

Also, it was a trial arising from natural affection. In prescribing the trial, God laid emphasis on this particular point, the natural affection and the love that Abraham felt for Isaac. 'Take now thy son, thine only son Isaac, whom thou lovest.'

Now the question might arise in the minds of some: 'Was it a correct statement that Isaac was Abraham's only son? Was not Ishmael also a son of Abraham?' Ishmael was indeed a son of Abraham, and in fact Abraham had a trial in connection with him also. God commanded Abraham to send Ishmael away, so that he would not be heir with Isaac. That was a great trial to Abraham. He prayed at one time, 'O that Ishmael might live before thee!' (Genesis 17:18). There again his natural affections were tried and yet he obeyed. He sent Hagar and Ishmael away—they no longer belonged to his family. So in that sense it was true, that now when this trial came, Isaac was his only son. (And of course Abraham had many sons after this, as we read later on. After the death of Sarah he married Keturah and he had sons.) But the emphasis is being laid on this son, Isaac—'thy son, thine only son Isaac, whom thou lovest'.

Abraham loved Isaac as his only son, the son of his old age, and he loved him as the son of Sarah. They themselves were heirs together of the life that shall never end, and Isaac was their child, and he was the child of promise (which was another aspect of the trial of Abraham's faith, and I shall come to deal with that in a moment). But what we are dealing with at the present is this trial in connection with Abraham's faith, the trial of natural affections being crossed, and being crossed in a most serious way. Hagar and Ishmael were sent away, and there was no doubt that Abraham's natural affections felt that, and he made it quite plain that he did feel it—but he was obedient. But this was a still more severe trial as far as natural affections were concerned. Here was this child, this son of his, Isaac, who was his only son. He was the only son he had in his tent, the son he saw when he rose up and when he lay down. His affections were very much set on Isaac. And now here was this trial of faith meeting with natural affection.

It is very often a great trial to faith, when the command of God and obedience to that command goes contrary to natural affection. There is absolutely no doubt that Abraham was deeply wounded in his soul when God said to him, 'thy son', then emphasised to him, 'thine only son, whom thou lovest'. Each of these statements must have been like arrows making wounds in the spirit of Abraham. This son of his—for whom he had waited so long and at whose birth he so greatly rejoiced—and now this command. 'Take thy son, and go into the land of Moriah, and offer him there for a burnt offering.' As you know, the burnt offering was first of all slain with a knife, and its blood was shed, and then its body was burnt to ashes. That was the prospect. That was the command given by God to Abraham. It was a command to take this son, his only son whom he loved, and to offer him up as a burnt offering; which meant slaying him with a knife, shedding his blood, and causing his body to be burnt to ashes. So I need not elaborate on this particular point, how painful this command was to the fatherly heart and the natural affection of this man of God. How many temptations he must have had in connection with it! How he must have wondered! Although we do not have any record of it, we can very well imagine Satan saying to him, 'Did God indeed say so? Did God indeed give such a command?' Well, he believed that God did, and now he was confronted with the nature of this trial. It was a trial with which his natural affections were very much bound up, and his natural affections painfully wounded. When that takes place then faith needs to be in a very strong exercise to overcome. We do not always appreciate the power of natural affection. We live in a generation in which a great deal of people do not even have natural affection. That is deplorable beyond words, and it is a mark of an evil generation and perilous times. But that was not the case with Abraham. The exercise of his faith in this particular aspect was that he looked above and beyond the pain of his natural affections to God's command, and he was obedient to it.

The trial of Abraham's spiritual experience
Now, of course that was only one element of the trial. We are also told here by the apostle, 'By faith Abraham, when he was tried, offered up Isaac: and he that had received the promises offered up his only begotten son, of whom it was said, That in Isaac shall thy seed be

called.' Here is something which goes outside the bounds of natural affection. We are now coming to the spiritual realm, Abraham's spiritual experience in connection with spiritual things. We are told that he 'received the promises'. Now, you remember that 'receiving the promises' does not just mean receiving the promise itself but receiving the fulfilment of the promise. In the birth of Isaac Abraham had received the fulfilment of the promise. He had exercised faith in that promise—he believed God. He had exercised hope against hope, regarding not his own deadness or the deadness of Sarah's womb, and he had seen the promise fulfilled. It was a great source of rejoicing to him to have received the promise—in the sense not only of God making a promise to him, but granting him the substance of the promise. That was something he would never forget.

And now he was being faced with this, that the child of the promise was to be taken and offered up. Do you see that not only his natural affections but also his spiritual affections were involved in this? How he had rejoiced! Not merely with a natural rejoicing which a father would have over the birth of a son, but he rejoiced spiritually because he received the fulfilment of the promise in the birth of Isaac. And where was that joy now gone? What was going to happen to the joy that he had when he came to this trial? The very one who had been the source of that joy in his birth, in the fulfilment of the promise, was now to be burnt to ashes. So it was a tremendous trial from that point of view.

The trial of Abraham's faith in the promise of the Messiah

And it was also a tremendous trial from another point of view. Bound up in the fulfilment of the promise in the birth of Isaac was another promise, a promise that was pointing to the future, in which God was saying, 'In thy seed shall all the nations of the earth be blessed.' 'That seed,' says Paul writing to the Galatians, 'was Christ.' And Abraham knew that, he understood that, his faith had grasped that. He looked on Isaac not only as his own son, in whom the substance of the promise had been fulfilled in his own spiritual and personal experience, but also as the line through which the Saviour would come—the

Saviour of a number that would be as the stars of the sky for multitude. The promise of the coming Messiah was bound up with Isaac. And now, instead of Isaac living, instead of Isaac having a seed, instead of Isaac having a family which would be propagated down through the generations, before there was any natural seed from him, from which the Messiah would eventually come, God's command was to offer him up as a burnt offering. So this was another element in the trial in a very powerful way as Abraham viewed Isaac. He knew that the promise of God with regard to Isaac was not only that he would come but that through him the nations of the world were to be blessed with the blessings of eternal life (the blessings of the life that Sarah and Abraham themselves had), and that 'in Isaac shall thy seed be called' and that seed was Christ. Yet now God's command was to take Isaac into the land of Moriah and on Mount Moriah (as I believe) to be offered up as a sacrifice, a burnt offering, burnt to ashes.

Abraham did not stumble

So what a trial to the faith of Abraham this was! What a mysterious trial! Yet he was assured that God had given this command to him. And therefore he must be obedient to it. And we see now how his faith was exercised in connection with that. He 'accounted that God was able to raise him up, even from the dead'. The words in the chapter in Genesis are very remarkable. When they came to the mount and saw the place afar off, Abraham said unto his young men, 'Abide ye here with the ass; and I and the lad will go yonder and worship, and come again to you.' I think these are very wonderful words: 'and come again to you'. He expected to come down from Mount Moriah and he expected that Isaac would be with him. Yes! Although Isaac would be slain and burnt to ashes, Abraham believed that the young men would see them both together again. So his faith was exercised in this way. He believed that this was God's command. He believed therefore that this would have to happen, that as God commanded Isaac would be slain and his body would be burnt to ashes. But he also believed that God was able to raise him up, even from the dead.

161

From these words we can see quite plainly that Abraham did believe in the resurrection of the dead. He was certain that that would take place at the end of time. Abraham did not believe that death was the end. He believed that there was, and could be, such a thing as a resurrection of the dead. And because he believed that, he also believed that God was able to raise Isaac from the dead. That's what his faith took hold of. Although it was a trial, he did not stumble at the idea that this was going contrary to the promise of God, in that the one in whom the promise of the Messiah was to be fulfilled was to be slain and his body burnt to ashes. His faith rose above the death of Isaac and looked to the power of God, that if God's promise was to remain true, Isaac would be raised from the dead. He went up the mountain, no doubt with a heavy heart and a heavy step and a cloud of sorrow round his mind, as far as his natural affections and also his spiritual affections were concerned. And yet at the same time he looked to the power of God. Although the altar would be built, and the wood put on the altar, and Isaac laid on the altar, and although he would use the knife he was taking up with him to slay his son and shed his blood, and although he would then set fire to the wood and burn his body to dust and ashes, yet he believed that God was able to raise him from the dead, and that he and Isaac would come down that mountain together! What wonderful faith it was! What great faith it was!

God's deliverance

As we know from the history, in actual fact Isaac was not slain. Before that took place the Lord—and we believe the Angel of the Lord to be the Lord himself—called to Abraham and said, 'Lay not thine hand upon the lad, neither do thou any thing unto him: for now I know that thou fearest God, seeing thou hast not withheld thy son, thine only son from me.' At that point when God spoke from heaven, as far as Abraham's soul was concerned, he had offered up Isaac. 'Thou hast not withheld thy son, thine only son.' Before he came to the actual act of putting Isaac to death, Abraham had offered him up. When Abraham took the knife in his hand to slay his son, as far as Abraham's will was concerned Isaac was gone, he was dead. As far as Abraham's will was concerned, he had given up his son, his only son whom he loved—he had given him up to God in obedience to God.

When the Angel of the Lord spoke from heaven and prevented him putting the knife on the lad, then he received him back from the dead. As far as his will was concerned Isaac was gone. But now, when the Lord told him not to lay his hand on the lad, he received Isaac back from the dead. 'From whence also he received him in a figure.' There was Isaac, on the altar, and the wood was there, the knife was in Abraham's hand, and as far as Abraham's will was concerned, Isaac was gone. But here was this intervention from heaven. And when Abraham stood back with the knife still in his hand and laid it aside, Isaac rose from off the altar, coming back from the dead, 'in a figure'. Perhaps it is not a good thing to imagine too much, but one cannot but think of the feelings of Abraham as he unbound Isaac his son and thus received him back from the dead. The faith of Abraham was tried and became triumphant. His faith triumphed because he believed in the power of God to raise the dead on that mount in the land of Moriah, the mountain on which the temple was to be eventually built hundreds of years after this. The Lord said, 'I know that thou fearest God, seeing thou hast not withheld thy son, thine only son from me.' Abraham's faith thus was triumphant in one of the greatest exercises of faith that ever took place in this world outside of the divine Redeemer himself.

God's blessing

In connection with that exercise of faith, the Lord then said to him (Genesis 22:16–18), 'By myself have I sworn, saith the Lord, for because thou hast done this thing, and hast not withheld thy son, thine only son: that in blessing I will bless thee, and in multiplying I will multiply thy seed as the stars of the heaven, and as the sand which is upon the sea shore; and thy seed shall possess the gate of his enemies; and in thy seed shall all the nations of the earth be blessed; because thou hast obeyed my voice.' In other words, the Lord was setting his seal on the promise of the coming Messiah, and he was setting his seal on it in the soul of Abraham in connection with this exercise of faith and the trial through which it went.

Now it is usual that when one of God's people has passed through a trial in connection with the exercise of their faith, they are brought to a wealthy place (Psalm 66:12). That's the wealthy place that Abraham was brought to—that God renewed and sealed in his spiritual experience the promise of the coming Messiah. Undoubtedly he rejoiced in that greatly. What peace and joy must have entered his soul when the Lord spoke to him in this way, when the Lord made known to him that he knew that he feared him, that he had the fear of God in his heart, which is the beginning of wisdom (or in other words, that he was a child of God), and when the Lord renewed the promise to him and sealed it more powerfully home on his heart!

Now I believe (and I think that this would be the general opinion of most who know about this passage) that Abraham never had a trial in connection with his faith again. He certainly did not have one of this nature, if you read the history after this. This trial through which he went brought him to a place where the Lord did not try his faith again. His natural feelings were of course affected in connection with the death of Sarah, and no doubt his spiritual union to Sarah too. How he felt it when he came to mourn for Sarah and to weep for her! But it wasn't a trial of his faith. In chapter 24, when we read, 'Abraham was old, and well stricken in age: and the Lord had blessed Abraham in all things,' the impression one gets is that he enjoyed a considerable amount of peace in his soul and in his spiritual experience in this world. In many ways that is what we would expect, and from the history one concludes that it is so.

That is often the case with God's people—not all of them, of course, as the trials of their faith are of varied descriptions, but very often it is the case that when a person passes through a particularly severe trial and they are blessed in it, then after that they have a period of considerable enjoyment of peace—that peace of which we read, 'Thou wilt keep him in perfect peace, whose mind is stayed on thee: because he trusteth in thee.' We should endeavour to learn from these things, at least that the possession of the grace of faith does not exclude us from trials—on the contrary, it means that we are often tried.

There is one last point I would like to mention in connection with this. The emphasis in the Scripture is put on the trial of Abraham's faith, but if you look at it you will see that he was also tried in connection with his love. 'Isaac whom thou lovest.' His love to Isaac and his love to God were put in the balance. He came down on the side of God, and he did not withhold. He saw that his love to God was greater than his love to Isaac, and that was a very wonderful thing too, as well as his faith. (And then of course he also had the grace of hope, but that is another subject altogether.)

Lessons to learn from Abraham's trial

We should seek to learn lessons from these cases, as we have been endeavouring to handle them as they arise in this chapter. We should be trying to get more and more light upon how the grace of faith is exercised in the experience of God's people. Although Abraham is an outstanding case, there are points which are similar, particularly that faith will cleave to the promise, and cleave to the power of God. When faced with trials, faced with difficulties, faced with trials bound up with natural affections and trials bound up with spiritual things, faith will not let go the promise, and faith will not let go of the fact that faithful is he who promised, who also will do it.

May he bless his Word.

14 Isaac

HEBREWS 11:20

By faith Isaac blessed Jacob and Esau concerning things to come.

WEDNESDAY, 28TH MARCH 1984

THE apostle, in describing the exercises of the grace of faith in the Old Testament saints, now comes to the case of Isaac, the son of Abraham. As we noticed, when Abraham received the commandment and was obedient to the commandment to offer up his son Isaac on Mount Moriah, it was an outstanding evidence of the exercise of the grace of faith overcoming the powers of natural affection. That was one aspect of the faith of Abraham, that although he loved his son, his only son Isaac—and God giving the commandment to him stressed the fact that it was his only son whom he loved—yet, in the exercise of faith, Abraham was enabled to overcome the powers of the natural affection that he felt for Isaac his son.

It was also true that there were other strands or elements in Abraham's trial, as I mentioned in the previous sermon. But I mention this one for a particular reason—it would appear, in the case of Isaac, that he was led away by his natural affection. That was very strange for a man who had faith. But nevertheless it does show that, even where faith is, there are weaknesses and infirmities bound up with the child of God in the world. This whole incident with respect to Isaac and Rebecca and Jacob and Esau is one in which Isaac, and also Rebecca (who also knew by revelation what was to become of the condition with regard to her sons), were led astray by infirmities, even though they had saving faith. It is of course true of the people of God in this world, that they are compassed about with infirmities. And even where the grace of faith is, these infirmities may lead them to act according to their infirmities and not according to the strength of faith.

Now as we were singing in Psalm 105, the promise made to Abraham was renewed to Isaac. That was the promise that through the line of Abraham, and in particular through the line of Isaac, the Messiah was eventually to come. That was clearly taught, as Paul mentions in his epistle to the Galatians with regard to the seed of Abraham—that seed was Christ, the Son of God, the Saviour of the lost and the undone. Isaac knew and believed it to be the case, through the covenant made with Abraham and renewed to him, that it was in this line that the Messiah was to come. And he also knew from the experience of Rebecca his wife that Jacob was the one through whom the Messiah was to come. He knew that, and he knew that by faith, and he understood that by faith.

Isaac's affection for Esau

Isaac was a good man, a godly man. We can get an insight into his piety from one of the names of God, that is, 'the fear of my father Isaac' (Genesis 31:42, 53). Isaac must have been one who had the fear of God in his heart, which is the beginning of wisdom. Isaac also had the grace of God in his heart and the faith which acts on the Word of God.

Now despite all that, it was equally well the case that Isaac had great affection for his elder son Esau. That, of course, was natural affection for his son Esau. We know that Esau had been a grief to him. We read that 'Esau was forty years old when he took to wife Judith the daughter of Beeri the Hittite, and Bashemath the daughter of Elon the Hittite: which were a grief of mind unto Isaac and to Rebekah' (Genesis 26:34–35). Isaac had grief of mind in connection with the conduct of Esau taking these wives. It was a pain and a sorrow to him that one who belonged to the tribe of Israel would turn aside in this way to choose these wives. That showed how evident and plain it was that Esau was not a spiritually-minded man but a worldly-minded man, and that he was very much taken up with the things of the world. In fact, as we know, he was prepared to sell his birthright for a mess of pottage. He gave the greatest evidence, evidence that was clear and decided, that he was of the earth, earthy. And yet his father—godly man though he was—very evidently had a great affection for Esau. That shows how, even where grace is and the grace of faith and the fear of God is, how powerful natural affection may be and very often is.

This is one of the great contrasts between Isaac and Abraham his father. In the case of Abraham, his love to Isaac was not only natural affection but also spiritual affection. Isaac was the child of the promise and no doubt the very fact that Isaac was so willing to be obedient to his father in connection with the sacrifice that was to be made on Mount Moriah indicated that Isaac himself had saving grace in his heart. So Abraham's love to Isaac was love to one who, in his young days, manifested himself to be altogether worthy of the love of such a father. But not so Esau. Esau was a source of grief and sorrow to Isaac.

But Isaac had a great natural affection for his elder son. So when Isaac was old and his eyes were dim, when he was beginning to close his eyes on the world and he knew that he was drawing near the end of life's journey, he was to exercise that which belonged to him as a parent in blessing his son and conveying the family blessing to his son. That is what he intended to do. 'I know not the day of my death,' he said (Genesis 27:2), and so he desired that his soul would bless Esau before he died. That was surely a very strange thing when he knew very well that the blessing was to go to Jacob. But here you have the power of natural affection, and it is very powerful indeed. The ties of flesh and blood, the ties of a father for his son, are very powerful indeed. We can see that although he knew and understood, even from the experience of his wife, that Jacob was the one to whom the blessing was to go, yet at the same time, facing the solemnity of death and eternity, he was disposed to bless Esau.

We also get an indication in the narrative of one of the ways in which the natural affection of Isaac was drawn out to Esau. He said to him, 'Go out to the field, and take me some venison; and make me savoury meat, such as I love, and bring it to me, that I may eat; that my soul may bless thee before I die' (Genesis 27:3–4). Esau's prowess as a hunter and his being able to capture meat and prepare it for his father all strengthened the natural and powerful affection that Isaac felt for his elder son. It may very well be the case that a son, being loved by his father, may strengthen that love by doing a particular thing which is pleasing to the father. Isaac's infirmity here was that he overlooked the fact that Esau was a graceless and a godless man even though he showed kindness to his father in preparing for him this savoury meat.

Isaac was deceived

We see in the narrative that Rebecca also knew that the blessing was to go to Jacob. She knew that by divine revelation, and she believed that. And when she overheard what Isaac said to Esau, she exhibited another frailty—that of seeking to see the Word of God fulfilled in a way that was inconsistent with proper conduct. She entered into a scheme with her son Jacob, to deceive Isaac her husband so that the blessing would come to Jacob. That again was clear evidence of frailty on Rebecca's part, that, although she had faith, she would stoop to this form of conduct. No doubt she would be making many excuses to herself. She could say, 'Well, my husband Isaac, he's blind, he doesn't know what he's doing. He's old, he's forgotten that the promise is to come to Jacob and I must put things right.' But the method she adopted was not right. It was a method of deceit. It was a bringing about the fulfilment of the promise of God to Jacob in a way that was not consistent with upright conduct. It is a great weakness and a great frailty in anyone who has the grace of faith, that they would indulge in this kind of way to seek to make the promise of God effective by putting their own hand deceitfully into the operation of the providence of God. Instead of Rebecca waiting on God and his providence, and believing that God would bring it about that the blessing would come to Jacob, whatever Isaac did or did not do, she introduced her own carnal wisdom and her own carnal activities into the event, and Jacob cooperated with her.

Now one would have thought that there would have been checks of conscience. And I would say that one of the great checks of conscience, which Jacob must have felt particularly, was when he brought in the food to Isaac and said, 'I am Esau thy firstborn; I have done according as thou badest me: arise, I pray thee, sit and eat of my venison, that thy soul may bless me. And Isaac said unto his son, How is it that thou hast found it so quickly, my son? And he said, Because the Lord thy God brought it to me' (Genesis 27:19–20). Isaac's question ought to have gone into Jacob's conscience. I have no doubt it did, to some extent, and yet this is what he said, 'Because the Lord thy God brought it to me.' What a sad answer he gave! He knew perfectly well that he had not been out hunting at all, that it had just been taken out of the flock and given to his mother to prepare, and yet he would speak in this pious way to his father to encourage the movement of events! Surely also he must have felt a check of conscience when he kissed his father. He came near to his father in this way and heard his father saying, as he smelled his raiment, 'See, the smell of my son is as the smell of a field which the Lord hath blessed!'

Isaac gave the blessing

Then Isaac proceeded to give the patriarchal blessing, and he did that by faith. We must notice here how the sovereignty of God is exercised, and the overruling of God. Despite all these frailties on the part of Isaac, on the part of Rebecca and on the part of Jacob, there was no question whatsoever of the promise failing. That could not be. Isaac proceeded to bless Jacob. He blessed him by faith—that is, looking to the promise of God—and he blessed him with respect to things to come. 'By faith Isaac blessed Jacob and Esau concerning things to come.' The exercise of faith does not take to do with the things that are seen but the things which are unseen. Although in this particular case the blessing was undoubtedly granted through the Spirit of prophecy, it was nevertheless a blessing that took to do not with the things which are seen but the things which are unseen. In this particular case they were unseen because they were future, but the principle is the same in every exercise of faith. The blessing he gave was, 'God give thee of the dew of heaven, and the fatness of the earth, and plenty of corn and wine: let people serve thee, and nations bow down to thee: be lord over thy brethren, and let thy mother's sons bow down to thee: cursed be every one that curseth thee, and blessed be he that blesseth thee' (Genesis 27:28–29). Over and above the temporal blessings, this embraced the promise to Abraham that 'in Isaac shall thy seed be called'. This nation was secured, and this blessing was secured, that through the line of Jacob the Messiah was to come.

When this blessing was given, it was done irrevocably. It could not be recalled. It could not be altered. The blessing had departed from Esau, it had descended on the head of Jacob. But now Esau came in from hunting and he too made savoury meat. Isaac was astonished at the situation which cropped up here. He trembled very exceedingly and said, 'I have blessed him' (that is, Jacob), and he goes on to say, 'Yea, and he shall be blessed' (Genesis 27:33). Although Isaac now knew exactly what had happened, and he knew he had been deceived, he knew that this blessing was irrevocable and that it could not and would not be recalled. But when Esau realised what had happened, he was in great grief and in great sorrow. 'Bless me, even me also, O my father!' 'Hast thou not reserved a blessing for me?' (Genesis 27:34–36). Esau wished to be blessed—but the blessing was gone, irrevocably. And Esau's grief and sorrow is referred to by the apostle when he says that Esau sought a 'place of repentance', and did not find it, 'though he sought it carefully with tears'. These words do not mean that Esau sought a place to repent of his sins. What it means is that he sought to make his father repent of having given the blessing to Jacob. He sought it with tears, as we have it in these very sad words, 'When Esau heard the words of his father, he cried with a great and exceeding bitter cry, and said unto his father, Bless me, even me also, O my father!' Those who seek a place of repentance in the sense of seeking to repent of their sins will find a place of repentance—but Esau sought repentance on the part of his father Isaac, that he would recall the blessing. But the blessing was irrevocable and could not be recalled. Isaac knew that, and that is what he said: 'I have eaten of all before thou camest, and have blessed him. Yea, and he shall be blessed.'

Esau was nevertheless given a blessing. But it was not the blessing in connection with the covenant—that was what Jacob had. But there was a blessing in connection with worldly goods and worldly prosperity, and this blessing was granted to Esau. But that is different from the blessing which Jacob received, the blessing in connection with the covenant of grace (for the covenant made with Abraham was a dispensation of the covenant of grace).

Lessons to learn from this event
Now the great lesson to be learned here first of all is that there are occasions when the people of God, though they possess the grace of faith, are encompassed with infirmities. These are things that they should be careful about. They should be careful with regard to natural affections, because being moved by natural affections, as happened here, was what dimmed the exercise of Isaac's faith. Then they should also be very careful, when they are trying to get a promise fulfilled, that they don't bring in carnal wisdom. Carnal wisdom will find plenty reason for acting in a way that is not in accordance with uprightness or truth. Rebecca suffered for what she did. She was afraid that she would lose both her sons in one day, and she did. Esau had nothing more to do with the covenant and she had to send Jacob away to a far country. And Jacob himself had to suffer many things in connection with that particular event, and had to be faced with the threat of Esau taking his life. Whatever the nature of the troubles may be, we can be quite sure that where a gracious person gives place to carnal reason, and especially in seeking to fulfil the promise of God, then there will be trouble. That person *will* run into trouble, because God will not honour carnal reason. He honours faith, the faith that waits on him with expectation.

The second great lesson we need to learn is about the sovereignty of God. 'The counsel of the Lord / doth stand for ever sure' (Psalm 33:11). Even the frailties of his own people and their bringing in their own carnal wisdom will not change the purpose of God. That purpose shall 'from age to age endure' (Psalm 33:11). Failings by Abraham and Sarah, and Isaac and Rebecca, and also Jacob—all these failings in connection with the people of God, bound up with the fact that they still had the remnants of sin in them, and the carelessness and lack of watchfulness on their part—none of these will cause that the promise of God will not be fulfilled, for his powerful purposes endure from age to age.

We also see once more that faith takes to do with things which are unseen. Isaac did not know the things which were to come until these things were revealed and made known to him and contained in the blessing, and in particular the blessing in connection with the covenant made with Abraham—the blessing of a coming Messiah and the blessing of salvation bound up with him. You remember Jacob's blessing too—he blessed his sons through the Spirit of prophecy, and in the exercise of faith with regard to the things that were to happen to his children in the latter day. This is the wonder of faith—it takes to do with the things that are unseen. Although the Spirit of prophecy is no longer works in this way, yet faith takes to do with the Word of God. What God has revealed in his Word, that is what faith lives on. Introducing carnal reason, instead of living in the exercise of faith, weakens faith. Faith's grasp of the Word of God is weakened by carnal reason, and then they go astray and these infirmities encompass them.

The lessons the Word of God teaches us are lessons that we should endeavour to learn. We should be constantly on the watchtower with regard to all the movements of our hearts and all the movements of our souls. We should be very careful that we live a life of faith. If we have grace, we should be very careful to cleave to the Word of God and avoid introducing carnal reason and carnal methods, saying to ourselves that we are just doing this so that God's Word might be fulfilled. That is not the way it will be fulfilled, but the Lord fulfils in his own time. 'Wait on the Lord, and be thou strong, / and he shall strength afford / unto thine heart; yea do thou wait, / I say, upon the Lord' (Psalm 27:14).

May he bless his Word.

15 Jacob

HEBREWS 11:21
By faith Jacob, when he was a dying, blessed both the sons of Joseph; and worshipped, leaning upon the top of his staff.

WEDNESDAY, 4ᵀᴴ APRIL 1984

ON the last occasion we were considering the fact that Isaac blessed Jacob and Esau concerning things to come, and this was an exercise of faith. Now Jacob was coming to the end of life's journey, and he blessed both the sons of Joseph his son. As has been emphasised in the chapter all along, the people of God live a life of faith upon the Son of God, and also, when they come to die, they die in the exercise of faith.

Jacob exercised faith at this particular time, 'when he was a dying'. It is evident from how he 'worshipped, leaning upon the top of his staff', that his bodily strength was almost gone. As we were reading in Genesis chapter 48, he was now old in years, his eyesight was gone, he was sick, drawing nigh the gates of death. But although that was the case, the weakness of his body did not mean that his faith was weakened. So this is part of the lesson that we are called on to learn with regard to this particular instance—that when Jacob was frail, when he was sick, when he was drawing near the end of life's journey, when the tabernacle of the body was getting ready to fall to the ground, yet faith was still in living and lively exercise in his soul. So, like his father Isaac, like his grandfather Abraham, like the others whose cases we have been considering already, he lived a life of faith, and when he came to die, he died in faith. 'These all died in faith.' And 'he worshipped, leaning upon the top of his staff—he was engaged in an act of worship when he exercised faith in this particular way.

Joseph brought his two sons, Ephraim and Manasseh, to Jacob in order that they might receive the blessing of this eminent man of God, his own father. These sons had been born, not in the land of promise, but in the land of Egypt. Jacob himself notices this when he says, 'Thy two sons, Ephraim and Manasseh, which were born unto thee in the land of Egypt before I came unto thee into Egypt.' He also says, 'They are mine; as Reuben and Simeon, they shall be mine' (Genesis 48:5). They were to be numbered among the tribes of Jacob. He also said to Joseph, 'I had not thought to see thy face' (Genesis 48:11). As you remember, Joseph was sold into Egypt and Jacob had come to the conclusion that he would never see his son Joseph again—that he had been killed, and that that was the end. But when word was brought to him that Joseph was yet alive, he made up his mind to go down to Egypt to see him before he died. 'I had not thought to see thy face: and, lo, God hath shewed me also thy seed.'

By faith Jacob blessed the lads

We read that 'Israel stretched out his right hand, and put it upon Ephraim's head, although he was the younger, and his left hand upon Manasseh's head, guiding his hands wittingly' (Genesis 48:14). Jacob was doing it wittingly. He could not do it with his natural eyesight, because his eyesight was dim. But by the secret impulse of the Spirit of God he put his right hand on Ephraim's head and his left hand on Manasseh's. So here the primary blessing came upon Ephraim although he was the younger, and the lesser blessing upon Manasseh.

Blessing them in this way, we are told, was an exercise of faith. There is no exercise of faith but by the Spirit of God. We are told in the Scripture that 'it is God which worketh in you both to will and to do of his good pleasure' (Philippians 2:13). The Holy Spirit works the grace of faith in the soul of a sinner—and he does that as his own gift—and that faith needs to be strengthened with regard to the exercise of it. Although the Holy Spirit implants the grace of faith in the souls of his people, and that grace of faith can never be lost, yet it can never be exercised apart from the gracious power of the Holy Spirit enabling the soul. It is not put into the soul and then it's left to the soul to exercise that faith in a kind of mechanical way. Faith must be exercised by the power of the Holy Spirit on every occasion. As the Saviour said to his disciples, 'Without me ye can do nothing' (John 15:5)—and that is true with regard to the exercise of the grace of faith, as it is true with regard to every exercise of soul.

Jacob viewed God as the covenant God

Now in blessing them in the exercise of faith, Jacob mentions here three ways in which he views the one in whose name he blessed them. The first is, is 'the God before whom my fathers Abraham and Isaac did walk' (Genesis 48:15). That is the mention he makes of God. The grace of faith is dependent on the Lord revealing himself and it exercises itself with respect to the knowledge that the soul possesses of God. That is what happened here. The eye of Jacob's faith was on this person, 'the God before whom my fathers Abraham and Isaac did walk'. His faith was on the covenant God of Israel, the God who had promised them the seed which in the fulness of the times would come (Galatians 4:4), the seed which Paul said was Christ (Galatians 3:16). The Old Testament saints were enabled by faith to embrace that promise and to rest their souls on Christ for time and for eternity. That was true of Abraham and Isaac, and it was also true of Jacob.

Jacob viewed God as the God who fed him

Jacob also mentions God in another way: 'the God which fed me all my life long unto this day' (Genesis 48:15). The faith of Jacob was also exercised in this way, that he had as the object of his faith 'the God which fed me all my life long unto this day'. That was true first of all with respect to the providence of God. As you remember, when the famine came, Joseph had been sent before Jacob and the rest of his brethren down to Egypt. God saw that there would be seed and food for Jacob and his family. And no doubt what is also involved here is the Lord was pleased to feed that seed in order that they might be preserved, because it was through that seed that the promised Messiah was to come. But also this was true with respect to spiritual feeding. In referring to God in this way, 'the God which fed me all my life long unto this day', Jacob is including not only the providential food with which he was fed for the upholding of his body but also the fact that he was fed in his soul by the Word of God, by the promises of the Word of God. He was fed and upheld in the faculties of his soul. This is always true with regard to the grace of faith. As we read in the book of Psalms (81:10) the Lord said, 'I am the Lord thy God, which did / from Egypt land thee guide; / I'll fill thy mouth abundantly, / do thou it open wide.' The invitation to the exercise of faith is that the mouth of faith should be opened so that the Lord would feed the soul, and feed the soul by his Word, so that the soul would be of those of whom we read, that man—and particularly those who are spiritually-minded—would not live by bread alone, but by every word that proceedeth out of the mouth of God (Matthew 4:4).

When Jacob blessed Joseph and his two sons, he exercised faith with respect to the fact that God had preserved him up till the present time in his providence, and supplied all his needs. He saw that to be out of the mercy and the kindness and the love and the favour of God. He did not consider that he had a right to the bread that he fed on. He recognised that he had forfeited every right—to every temporal blessing as well as every spiritual blessing—by reason of sin. But by the grace of faith, when he views the providential provision that God gives the soul, the sinner acknowledges God. He acknowledges him in all his ways—that he is the God who has fed him 'all my life long unto this day'. And he acknowledges that God is the one who feeds him spiritually, the one who provides him with the heavenly manna, with the bread of life which came down from heaven. 'My Father giveth you this bread,' said the Saviour (John 6:32), and that bread is Christ revealed in the Word of God. That's the food on which Jacob fed, and Isaac and Abraham—the promise of the Messiah who was to come.

Jacob viewed God as the Redeemer

In this exercise of faith Jacob goes on to say, 'The Angel which redeemed me from all evil, bless the lads' (Genesis 48:16). Here is the third view by faith that he has of the Lord. He calls him 'the Angel which redeemed me from all evil'. This view of God was made known to Jacob in a special way at Luz, which was afterwards called Bethel, where he fell asleep and where he was granted a dream in which he saw the ladder stretching up from earth to heaven, and the angels of God ascending and descending on that ladder. He said, 'Surely the Lord is in this place,' and he called the name of the place Bethel, the house of God (Genesis 28:16, 19), and it was then that the Lord promised him that he would be with him whithersoever he went. So he came to see a ladder from earth to heaven. It was revealed and made known to him that this was the way from earth to heaven—the ladder from earth to heaven, and the angels of God ascending and descending on that ladder.

Then the years passed by, and the promise was fulfilled and the Saviour came into the world. And when he was in the world we read of a man called Nathaniel, who was called by Philip to come to the Saviour. When he came to the Saviour, the Saviour said to him, 'Because I said unto thee, I saw thee under the fig tree, believest thou? thou shalt see greater things than these. And he saith unto him, Verily, verily, I say unto you, Hereafter ye shall see heaven open, and the angels of God ascending and descending upon the Son of man' (John 1:50–51). Now the question may be asked, 'What was Nathaniel doing under the fig tree?' We are not told specifically, but we can come to a conclusion from the words of the Saviour when he said of Nathaniel, 'Behold an Israelite indeed, in whom is no guile!' (John 1:47). When we turn to Psalm 32 we know that the man 'in whose spirit there is no guile' is a man who is confessing his sin. Now, I believe that that was what Nathaniel was doing under the fig tree. With the eye of Christ on him, and no other eye, he was there confessing his sins. And the Saviour said that he was to see this great sight, 'heaven open, and the angels of God ascending and descending upon the Son of man'. So the vision that was granted to Jacob was a vision of a ladder from earth to heaven, and that ladder was the Son of Man. That is the implication of what Christ says.

The Redeemer is the ladder between earth and heaven

Now when Jacob came to Bethel, he was an outcast from his father's house, and his own sins and follies had brought him to that state. We have no doubt that when he came to Bethel, he was like Nathaniel, confessing his sins. All those who are taught by the Spirit of God to confess their sins, they confess them from a realisation that by reason of these sins they have closed the door to heaven, they have closed the door to God's favour on themselves. They understand that. It is clear to them that they have sinned against heaven and in God's sight, and that the door to God's favour and blessing has been closed on them by their own sins until they come to view by faith the way to heaven that has been opened, and that the way to heaven is this ladder, the Son of Man.

He is first of all a ladder in the sense that he is the Son of Man—he is the Son of God and the Son of Man. Christ is the way, the truth and the life. 'No man cometh unto the Father but by me' (John 14:6). He is a ladder to heaven in respect of the fact that in him the nature of God and the nature of man meet together in the person of Emmanuel, God with us.

But Jacob also mentions another sense in which the Saviour is the ladder to heaven, and that is the phrase that he uses here, 'the Angel which redeemed me from all evil'. That Angel was Christ, the divine Redeemer. He is the ladder and the way to heaven, not only because he is the Son of God in our nature but because he is the Redeemer. That's how heaven is opened. That's how the ladder stretches from earth to heaven—not only because Christ is the Son of God and the Son of Man in one glorious person, but because he is the Redeemer, who has opened a new and a living way and consecrated a new and a living way through the rent veil of his flesh, through his body being broken and his blood being shed for the remission of the sins of many. He opened the way, as you remember, when he cried on the cross, 'It is finished!' He gave that great cry. That happened outside the city of Jerusalem. Inside the temple, inside Jerusalem, the hand of God tore the veil between the holy place and the most holy place. It was rent from the top to the bottom, so that the way into the holiest of all was now made manifest.

And so the Saviour as the God-Man and as the Redeemer is the ladder and the way to heaven. He is the one, because his body was rent, because his soul was bruised, because his blood was shed for the remission of the sins of many. And now heaven is open—it is open to the soul that comes by this new and living way. It is a clear mark of faith, wherever it is, that the object of faith is not only Christ in his person (although that is embraced in it), but Christ as the way to the Father—Christ is the ladder from earth to heaven. Through his death, Christ is the way in which the door of heaven, which was closed against the lost and ruined race of mankind on account of their sins, is now opened.

This was made known to Jacob, as it was made known to Nathaniel. It is made known to the sinner who is confessing his sins, who sees no help in man at all, who understands that he cannot deliver himself, that no man can deliver himself, that there is only one way. He comes to see and to understand that this is the way. This is the way to the Father and this is the way into everlasting life—through faith in the divine Redeemer. 'The Angel redeemed me from all evil'—from all evil! And from the greatest evil of all, the wrath and curse of God due to him on account of his sins. They have redemption through his blood, the forgiveness of sins, according to the riches of his grace.

This was Jacob's prayer and this was his blessing, that this Angel would bless the lads, and that he would bless them (I have no doubt whatsoever) in this particular way, in making known to them that he was the Redeemer. That is the meaning of the phrase, 'Let my name be named on them, and the name of my fathers Abraham and Isaac.' What name was that? Well, there's another reference to an Angel in connection with Jacob himself, and that is at Peniel, you remember, where he wrestled with the Angel, where he said, 'I will not let thee go except thou bless me.' The blessing wherewith the Angel of the Covenant blessed him was that his name was changed from Jacob, 'the supplanter', to Israel, 'the one who had power with God and with men', and who would prevail. That is the order that faith operates on. Esau was coming to meet Jacob, and Jacob was expecting that Esau would slay him, so he sent the cattle and so on over the river as a gift to Esau. But that wasn't the way that Esau was overcome at all. The way that Esau was overcome was by Jacob on his knees in Peniel, pleading with the Lord to protect him, pleading with the Angel to protect him from this evil. Because he had power with God at the throne of grace, he would have power with men also, to overcome the evil that was in the heart of his brother Esau.

Jacob refused Joseph's request

Now the next thing we notice here is, 'when Joseph saw that his father laid his right hand upon the head of Ephraim, it displeased him: and he held up his father's hand, to remove it from Ephraim's head unto Manasseh's head. And Joseph said unto his father, Not so, my father: for this is the firstborn; put thy right hand upon his head. And his father refused' (Genesis 48:17–19).

Although this was Joseph, Joseph his son, whom he loved as he loved no other son, Joseph the one to whom he gave the coat of many colours as a token of his love, Joseph the one who had saved his life (in the hand, undoubtedly, of the providence of God), yet, when Joseph came to interfere with what was spiritual, Jacob would not listen. He would have nothing to do with it. 'Not so,' says Joseph, and Jacob refused. Joseph was taking to do with something that was spiritual, something that had to do with what was to come, and what was to be fulfilled with respect to them. 'His father refused, and said, I know it, my son, I know it: he also shall become a people, and he also shall be great: but truly his younger brother shall be greater than he, and his seed shall become a multitude of nations. And he blessed them.'

When Jacob blessed them, he not only refused Joseph's request and deep-felt desire but, the Holy Spirit tells us, the children of Israel would observe the same order in the blessing in the days to come. 'In thee shall Israel bless, saying, God make thee as Ephraim and as Manasseh.' When it came to the spiritual realm, as we have mentioned already in connection with Abraham and in connection with Isaac, faith looks above and beyond the ties of natural affection and the ties of flesh and blood. I am sure that Jacob would have been very ready to grant anything that Joseph would ask him to do, because of the affection he had for Joseph and because of his indebtedness to Joseph, but when it came to the spiritual realm he refused it—it could not be so.

So again we see this evidence of the grace of faith, that when it comes to spiritual things the natural affections between a father and son are not allowed to interfere. That was true in the case of Abraham and Isaac, and in the case of Isaac with Jacob and Esau, and here you have the same thing being brought out in the case of Jacob and Joseph. And that's a great lesson, a tremendous lesson—that when it came to the spiritual realm, this man Jacob, in whom there was the grace of faith, refused his favourite son's request, and not only his request but his heartfelt desire. These two sons that were born in the land of Egypt, not in the land of promise, Joseph desired them to be blessed in a particular way, but Jacob refused it. This was the way of the Spirit of God, and it would be seen in the days to come.

Jacob looked ahead to the Promised Land

Now we come to the last thing that Jacob says here: 'Behold, I die: but God shall be with you, and bring you again unto the land of your fathers.' Here he is speaking in the Spirit of prophecy (as Joseph too was to do later on). He was assured of the fact that they would be delivered out of the land of bondage (as the land of Egypt was to become to them), and brought back to the Promised Land. As Jacob was blessing the sons of Joseph here, he had this knowledge that this would take place, that his sons would yet be mighty tribes in the land of Canaan. He believed the promise that had been given to Abraham that after 430 years, God would bring his people back from the land of Egypt and bring them to the land of Canaan.

Because Jacob was in possession of the grace of faith, when he had to say, 'Behold I die,' he was sure that although he would be gone— although the father of the tribes of Israel would be gone to eternity and they would see him no more—yet the God of Israel did not die, nor would the promise of the God of Israel fail. That is what Jacob is seeing here by faith.

How precious then is this grace of faith, during life and when death comes! And how necessary it is for us all to have this living faith, the faith that stands not in the wisdom of man but in the power of God, the spiritual faith wrought in the heart by the Holy Ghost in effectual calling!

May he bless his Word.

16 Joseph

HEBREWS 11:22
By faith Joseph, when he died, made mention of the departing of the children of Israel; and gave commandment concerning his bones.

DATE UNKNOWN, 1984

THE apostle, dealing with the various cases of patriarchs, now comes to the case of Joseph. He stresses the fact that Joseph made manifest his faith in particular when he died. Just as it was true in the case of Jacob that he manifested his faith when he was dying, so it was true of Joseph. All these servants of God had also manifested their faith in their life. In their own way, they passed through many different dispensations and trials and tribulations of one kind and another. And in the midst of these dispensations and trials one thing was very evident with regard to them all, and that was how their faith came into living exercise on these occasions. Abraham when he was tried offered up Isaac, and manifested his faith in that way, the faith that worketh by love. And when they came to the greatest trial of all, that is, to face death, to leave this world forever and to pass into eternity, they manifested their faith when they were dying: 'these all died in faith'. They all died in faith, and the Holy Spirit stresses the fact that they died in faith, in the exercise of faith, in different ways.

Now we come to Joseph, this eminent man of God. We are told that when he died, he died in faith. He manifested that faith by making mention of the departing of the children of Israel, and he manifested the certainty of his faith by giving commandment concerning his bones. As I have been endeavouring to stress, it is very important that we all understand that the exercise of faith has in view, in an outstanding and particular way, the promise of God. Faith is that grace which feeds on God's promise. The object of faith is the promise of God and what the promise of God contains. This was true of Joseph when he died.

Joseph's faith had been tried

We know from the history of Joseph that he was not only an eminent man of God, but he also rose to an eminent place in the land of Egypt. He was betrayed by his brethren, as we read in Genesis chapter 37, and he passed through great trials with regard to that, as we were reading and singing in Psalm 105: 'Joseph, whom unnaturally / sell for a slave did they.' When it was revealed to him that he was to have a place above his brethren, they sold him into Egypt, where he came into the house of Potiphar and after the incident there he found himself in prison (unjustly, as we know). And far from the word and purpose of God being fulfilled in connection with him, the very opposite appeared to be the case—he was under the heel of his enemies. That was a great trial, as the Word of God tells us. 'The word and purpose of the Lord / did him in prison try' (Psalm 105:19). I just want to stress this point, that the providence of God working in this way, landing Joseph in prison, tried his faith with respect to the word and purpose of the Lord. He was tried in connection with God's promise to himself, and God's purpose revealed in his promise to himself.

Joseph saw the promise of God fulfilled

Now, Joseph came to see, as he tells his brethren, that his betrayal, his landing in prison, all these events—God meant it unto good (Genesis 50:20). The purpose of God was to be fulfilled in a way that would be not only for the good of Joseph but for the good of the seed of Israel and their preservation in the midst of famine—'to save much people alive.' In these times of trial and desolation the faith of Joseph was

186

tried. He could see that in his situation, the word and purpose of God was not being fulfilled in the way that he would have expected. That is very often the case with regard to God's people—the events in their experience seem to be contrary to what they might have expected. It is a common source of trial to the grace of faith, that many of the expectations they had are crossed in their experience in the world. Their expectations are not realised and the word and purpose of God tries them.

There was that aspect to the faith of Joseph. But he lived to see the word and the purpose of God being fulfilled in a most remarkable way. He was raised up, as you remember, to Pharaoh's right hand, and he had control in the kingdom of Egypt. Eventually his father and his brethren and the seed of Israel came down to the land of Goshen, where they were under his care. He saw there the word of God and the purpose of God fulfilled in connection with himself.

Joseph exercised faith when he came to die

Therefore when he came to die, one would think that his faith had been wonderfully strengthened by what had happened in connection with himself and in connection with the preservation of his race. But when he came to die we discover that that is not what was exercising the mind of Joseph. It is not the prosperous state he had, it is not the high position he had, it is not how he had been vindicated in the providence of God from the enmity of his brethren—these things were not prominent in the eyes of Joseph when he was coming to die. Nor was he concerned as to how he would dispose of his possessions, or even so much with the fact of how he was dying and leaving empty his position of power and usefulness to the people of Israel in his day and generation.

'And Joseph said unto his brethren, I die' (Genesis 50:24). It was bad news to them that the one who was their protector and their shield was to die. They did not know what was going to happen to them when he was taken away. But Joseph knew what was going to happen to them because he knew, from the promise that was given to Abraham (Genesis 15), that God would deliver them with a great

187

deliverance once they fell under the power and bondage of their enemies in the land of Egypt. They were to sojourn in that land for a period of time, then the land of Egypt would become to them the land of bondage. Joseph believed what was revealed to Abraham. And when Joseph was dying, that was before his mind. Although he saw his children and his grandchildren brought up on his knees and God granting prosperity towards himself and his preservation of the tribes of Israel in the midst of the famine, yet he was also fully aware of the time of trial that stretched out before the people he was leaving behind. These people were where the cause of Jehovah was, where the promise of the Messiah was, where the church of God was. Joseph saw that, he understood that. He knew what was going to take place. Therefore what he had in view as he died was the strengthening of his brethren, the strengthening of the tribes of Israel, and that was by demonstrating the exercise of his own faith.

It is the case with both the cause of God and the individual people of God in the world, in both the Old Testament and the New Testament, that it is through great tribulation that they enter the kingdom (Acts 14:22). This is something that belongs to the kingdom of Christ, as we read in connection with those who, with the palms of victory in their hand, washed their robes and made them white in the blood of the Lamb—they were those who had come out of great tribulation (Revelation 7:14). And Christ himself told his people, 'In the world ye shall have tribulation' (John 16:33). The Lord's people experience tribulation as they pass through the wilderness of time to the promised land of heaven. Joseph knew the revelation that was given to Abraham—he did not know from direct revelation given to himself, but he believed the revelation that God had given to Abraham. He believed what God had said to Abraham, that his seed were to be in the land of strangers, and that they were to be 430 years. 'I die,' he said, 'but God will surely visit you, and bring you out of this land unto the land which he sware to Abraham, to Isaac, and to Jacob' (Genesis 50:24). He believed that God would visit them with his salvation, delivering them out of the land of Egypt, the house of bondage, and bringing them into the Land of Promise. In other words, he believed that the promise of God would be fulfilled.

And Joseph when he was dying had his eye on that promise for his brethren, not only for himself, because as a matter of historical fact he was not to experience it. But he was grieved for his brethren for the afflictions that they were to pass through. He knew these afflictions were destined for them to pass through, but he also knew that these afflictions were to have an end. 'The troubles that afflict the just / in number many be; / but yet at length out of them all / the Lord doth set him free' (Psalm 34:19). And 'he carefully his bones doth keep' (verse 20). That was to be fulfilled here in a very remarkable way with regard to Joseph himself.

So this is what Joseph's faith is resting on. He knows, he believes, that a time of furnace trial is coming to the church of God, but he believes equally well that God will visit them. Therefore he has brought them around him to hear what he has to say when he dies. 'And Joseph said unto his brethren'—that is, not only to his own near brethren but to his brethren in the tribes of Israel. He was saying this to the people he was leaving behind as his soul was to depart from his body. As he was leaving them behind, he was giving them this consolation, that God would visit them, that he would bring them out of the time of trial and out of the time of tribulation, and bring them to the Promised Land. Joseph believed that and he did not remain silent about it. He believed it and he witnessed to it publicly. His faith did not fall short on the public witness as to what he believed. When he was dying this was his last public witness to the faith that he possessed, his last public witness with respect to the promise given to Abraham, the last public witness to the fact that he was sure that God would fulfil his promise with regard to the children of Israel.

Joseph gave commandment concerning his bones

Faith face to face with death, when it is in living exercise, has a hope of the better country. No doubt Joseph himself had this comfort and consolation in his soul, that he was going to the better country, the rest that remaineth for the people of God. That is what his hope was.

He believed that when his soul left his body, he could say as surely as Paul did, that 'absent from the body' meant to be 'present with the Lord' (2 Corinthians 5:8). The Lord will be with his people in the valley of the shadow of death and will bring them out on the other side of death, and will bring them into the Father's house. The Lord's people have this faith in the promise of God, the promise of Christ, who said, 'I will never leave thee nor forsake thee' (Hebrews 13:5), and who also said, 'I go to prepare a place for you. And if I go and prepare a place for you, I will come again, and receive you unto myself; that where I am, there ye may be also' (John 14:2–3). That promise, they believe, will be fulfilled, and it is fulfilled when they die. And undoubtedly, although it may not always be the case, it is a thing to be desired, that they would be able to give this witness on their deathbed. I knew of a godly man, an elder in our church, who told a close friend of his that he was praying that he would have a bright deathbed, because he felt that so many of the Lord's people in our day did not have that, and he wanted it for the sake of his family and his friends. That was his desire and his prayer, and no doubt it was a proper desire and a proper prayer. That was what Joseph had here when he said to his brethren, 'I die'—he was dying a bright death, in the hope of eternal life, and not only so but also in the hope of the preservation of the cause of Christ and the cause of Jehovah.

It was because of that hope that 'he gave commandment concerning his bones'. 'And Joseph took an oath of the children of Israel, saying, God will surely visit you, and ye shall carry up my bones from hence' (Genesis 50:25). Joseph was embalmed, he was put in a coffin in Egypt, and his bones were to be preserved as they were in the land of Egypt until the time would come when God's promise would be fulfilled. Then this would take place, that the children of Israel would be brought out of the land of Egypt and they would carry the bones of Joseph with them. Joseph took an oath with regard to this, and that indeed did happen. They carried his bones with them and buried them in Canaan in the days of Joshua, as we read later on in the history.

That must have been a great comfort to those who were left behind when Joseph died. We have no doubt that they felt their loss greatly. We read of the mourning they had in connection with Jacob, and no doubt they mourned very much for their father Jacob. But also when it came to the case of Joseph, who had been a father to them in a very particular way as their protector, they mourned greatly then also. But Joseph gave commandment concerning his bones. He was assured that God would visit them. He was assured that they would be brought out of the land of Egypt, when it became a land of bondage to them, and brought to the Land of Promise. He put them on oath, saying, 'God will surely visit you, and ye shall carry up my bones from hence' (Genesis 50:25). He took an oath of the whole nation, the tribes of Israel who were to be delivered out of the land of bondage when God's time would come to fulfil his promise. 'He gave commandment concerning his bones' and so he was embalmed and 'he was put in a coffin in Egypt' (Genesis 50:26) until the time came when this visitation of salvation would take place.

Joseph's faith was strong

It shows us how strong was the faith of Joseph, how clear to his mind was the promise of God and the certainty of its being fulfilled—though he himself was not to see it, yet his people, the tribes of Israel would see it, and he was leaving this token with them, in this oath laid on them, that his bones would be carried up to the land of Canaan and buried there. But Joseph believed that after they passed through the time of trial, they would be brought to a wealthy place, they would be brought out of the land of Egypt, they would set their face upon the Promised Land, and they would enter into the land which he swore to Abraham, to Isaac, and to Jacob. Joseph believed that his own bones would be there and that they would bury them in the land there. That was indeed fulfilled in the days of Joshua after they had conquered the land and before Joshua died.

How strong then was the faith of Joseph, this eminent man of God! He had strong faith during his trials when the word and purpose of God tried him in prison, strong faith in the midst of all the trials,

191

and when he came to die his faith did not fail. Why? Because he kept his faith fixed on the promise of God. Although his body was to go into the dust, and although he was to die and leave his people and his children and his family and the cause of Christ behind, yet he knew that whatever loss the cause of Christ might have in its servants being taken away, that did not change the promise of God. All these promises will be fulfilled. And although it is, and properly, a cause of sorrow to the people of God when servants of Christ are taken away, yet that does not change the promise of God with regard to his cause and with regard to his kingdom. Although Joseph was going and although he had been so useful to the cause in his day and in his generation—few were more useful than he was, to preserve this people alive in the midst of famine and to preserve the cause of Christ in the midst of that desolation—yet he believed that his departing, his dying, did not for a single moment or in any way alter the promise of God.

Therefore it is of great importance for you and for me to have this faith wrought in our hearts. It is the gift of God, wrought in our hearts by the Holy Spirit through the Word of God, whereby we are united to Christ. Being united to Christ is of course to be united to the cause of Christ too, and to the people of God, and they are our companions and our friends, but it is important for us to recognise that it is through much tribulation they enter the kingdom. The Lord's people have tribulation appointed to them in this world. As Christ said, 'In this world ye shall have tribulation.' They have tribulations with regard to themselves, perhaps with regard to their families, with regard to their nation, with regard to the cause of Christ. These are some of the tribulations that they do have; but the promise of God will never fail. It does not fail. Tribulations do not make it fail. And faith will not fail where it is accompanied by prayer, and where it is accompanied by a spiritual understanding of the stability and the certainty of God's promise.

That is exemplified so wonderfully and so remarkably in the case of Joseph, as it was in others before him and others after him. 'Joseph, when he died, made mention of the departing of the children of Israel;

and gave commandment concerning his bones.' The eye of Joseph's faith was on the promise of God, and his assurance was that that promise would be fulfilled. It would be well for us if we had the like precious faith to be exercised through life and to be exercised at death.

May the Lord bless his Word.

17 Joseph's commandment

HEBREWS 11:22

By faith Joseph, when he died, made mention of the departing of the children of Israel; and gave commandment concerning his bones.

LORD'S DAY MORNING, 16TH DECEMBER 1979

IN the previous chapter the apostle has been exhorting the Hebrews not to cast away their confidence which hath great recompense of reward. They had been subjected to persecutions of one kind or another and they were tempted to turn back from the faith which they had professed. They were tempted to turn aside from following Christ through both good report and evil report. This epistle was largely written in order to strengthen their faith and to deliver them from casting away the confidence that they had.

The apostle points out that they needed not only faith but also patience. 'For ye have need of patience,' he said, 'that after ye have done the will of God ye might receive the promise,' which they received through faith. So that both faith and patience are needed with regard to receiving the fulfilment of the promise.

Then he goes on to say, 'The just shall live by faith, and if any man draw back, my soul shall have no pleasure in him.' First of all he goes on to speak of the nature of the grace of faith, and then he goes on to illustrate from the experience of the fathers under the Old Testament dispensation, how faith was made precious to them and how they were enabled to endure and to believe the promise and to expect the fulfilment of the promise. Nevertheless, as he said, they did not see the promise fulfilled in its full extent because that promise directed them to Christ who was still to come.

The apostle also says that faith is the substance of things hoped for. Here we have brought before us, not only the question of faith and patience, but also the fact that faith is the foundation for hope. It is the 'substance', it is that which stands under hope, and holds up hope and sustains hope and strengthens hope. Consequently the strength of our hope and the clearness of our hope is very largely dependent on the exercise of our faith. The apostle says here in connection with the things hoped for (that is to say, the things held out in the promises of God), that faith is the substance of them. Faith is what believes these promises and consequently it upholds the exercise of the grace of hope. Then it is the evidence of things hoped for, that the things which the eye hath not seen nor the ear heard, neither have entered into the heart of man, are brought near in the light of God's Word by the soul in the exercise of faith.

Now the apostle goes on to point out, although we must not spend time on this, that it is through faith that we understand that the worlds were framed by the word of God, so that the things which are seen were not made by things which do appear. This does not merely teach the doctrine of miraculous and divine creation, that God caused the earth to come into existence out of nothing, but it also teaches us that the things which were not seen, that is to say, the glories of God which could not be discerned unless God would manifest it, were made known in the works of creation. There was a revelation given in creation of that which man could not otherwise see, of the wisdom and the power and the Godhead of the God of eternity. When people speak about the world and the operations of laws in the world (or what we commonly call science in its various departments) they cannot receive the true essence and the true value of these things, however deeply they may penetrate into them, unless they have faith. That is something that we ought to remember. Human reason cannot discern the true glory of creation, or the true glory of what is manifested in creation. Paul teaches here not only that we believe that the worlds were framed by the word of God, but also that the things which are seen were not made by things which do appear, but that the invisible things of the glory of the nature of God, insofar as they are revealed in creation, are also made known to faith.

In connection with the various cases brought before us in this chapter, my mind was led on this occasion to Joseph. Joseph was a bright ornament in the church of God. Joseph was Jacob's favourite son, and his life is full of instruction for all those who desire to follow Christ. His life is full of instruction for all those who desire to overcome temptation by the strength of divine grace. Yet we are told here of his faith when he was dying. We might think that that is rather strange. We might think surely that there were other instances which could have been mentioned from his life. For instance, the apostle mentions from the life of Moses, how he refused to be called the son of Pharaoh's daughter, and so on. There are no doubt many things which could have been mentioned with regard to the life of Joseph, but no, this is what is mentioned—the exercise of his faith when he was dying.

The exercise of Joseph's faith in dying was a great evidence of the reality of his faith, a great evidence of how true it was that faith was the substance of things hoped for, that it is in the nature of faith to be, as Calvin calls it, the underlying prop to the grace of hope and to the things that are hoped for. In Joseph's case these things that were hoped for were things that he himself was not to see, such as God visiting his people and taking them out of the land of Egypt, and bringing them into the Land of Promise. Yet all these things he believed, and when he was dying in Egypt, and when he was dying in the midst of the glory of Egypt, this is what he was thinking of—not of the glory of Egypt, not even of the way that the Lord had honoured him, nor of the way that he had bound Pharaoh's princes and taught his senators wisdom (Psalm 105:22)—but all he thought of was the promise of God, and that in the very article of death.

1. Therefore we shall endeavour first of all to say something with regard to the time when Joseph's faith was exercised on this occasion, and that was when he died. He has now come to the end of life's journey, he is now going to say goodbye to faith and hope. These three graces had been in his soul, faith, hope and love, but he was now to enter into the experience that the greatest of these is charity, or love, and he was to say goodbye to faith and hope when he died.

2. In the second place we shall notice that his faith had to do with the promise of God with respect to the cause of Christ in the world. He was bidding goodbye to that also. He gathered his brethren round his bed, he told them that God was to visit them, that he was to bring them out of the land of Egypt, and that he was to bring them to the land he had promised to Abraham, Isaac and Jacob. He told this to his brethren, though he himself was leaving the earth, and though he himself would never see it. How touching it must have been too, that it was to his brethren that he said this, reminding them of the promise of God! Those who had betrayed him, those who had hated him, those who had rejected him, he was now gathering round his bed and he was telling them and reminding them of the promise of God.

3. And in the third place, we shall notice the commandment that he gave concerning his bones. He commanded that they would leave his bones in the land of Egypt, that he would not be buried with the great men and the kings of Egypt. Though he had been there during his lifetime, yet he desired to be buried with his fathers, in the Land of Promise. That's where he wanted his bones to be laid. By saying this he was assuring them of the promise of God. This commandment was not given to his brethren, but to Israel: it was given to the leaders of Israel, it was given to the people. He was not merely strengthening his brethren but he was strengthening the whole of Israel. When they left the land of Egypt, they left it with haste, in the night, under the shelter of the blood, having fed on the paschal lamb, with a staff in their hands and their loins girded. Yet they did not forget the bones of Joseph. They carried his bones with them, and they buried them in Shechem when they came into the land, as we read in the last verses

of the book of Joshua. What a wonderful thing this was! Here is a man dying. He's leaving the world, he's going to heaven to be with Christ, which is far better, he's going into the palace of the king, so far exceeding the glory of Pharaoh's palace as the heavens exceed the glory of the earth—yet he is remembering his bones, and he is desirous that they would be buried in a certain place, and desiring that when God would visit the children of Israel, they would not forget his bones. Though two hundred years were to pass before this would be fulfilled, they did not forget what Joseph had said to them. Moses did not forget, and neither did Joshua. When Moses was taken away, when he climbed the hills of Moab to Mount Pisgah and looked over Jordan and was taken away, Joshua carried this on, and the children of Israel carried it on, until they found a time of peace to bury Joseph's bones in Shechem.

1. The time when Joseph's faith was exercised

The first thing that we have brought before us is the time of this exercise of faith. It was when Joseph died. Nothing could be clearer than that Joseph believed that the death he was shortly to die involved the separation of his soul and his body. He spoke about his bones. He knew that his body would dissolve into dust—by the time that God was to visit Israel there would be nothing left but his bones. He is bringing before us clearly and unmistakably that he believed that temporal death was the separation of the body and the soul from one another. The sickle of death did this. This mysterious union between the soul and body, which none can understand, is broken in death. The sickle of death has power to cause a separation, and a separation that no other power can possibly cause. This is in the nature of death, that body and soul are separated from one another. But Joseph was dying in faith, and he was dying in the realisation that his body was to be left behind while his soul went into eternity.

Therefore Joseph was one of those of whom we read, 'Blessed are the dead that die in the Lord.' He was dying united to Christ, with respect both to his body and to his soul. The members of the body are members of Christ. The soul is redeemed and so is the body, as far as

God's people are concerned. Joseph was one of those blessed ones who 'die in the Lord'—who die united to Christ, who are in Christ as the branch is in the vine, and as each member of the body is in the body. They die 'in Christ' and united to him. When we read here, 'by faith Joseph, when he died', this points to the fact that the union between Christ and Joseph was a union by faith. Faith is the particular grace by which the soul and Christ are united to one another. Therefore when Joseph died in faith, united to Christ, he did so because this had taken place in his life—that he had come to exercise faith in Christ in the promise of God.

When Joseph gave commandment concerning his bones, he used these words, 'God shall visit you.' He used these words not only because he believed in God's promise to Abraham that after his people had been afflicted for four hundred odd years, he was to bring them out of the land of bondage. He also used these words because he knew he could not have had faith unless God had visited him. No one has faith as he is by nature. We all have natural faith—we trust people, we believe in people, we believe the things we read about in books, and so on. We all have faith and trust in that natural sense of the term. But no one by nature has the faith that unites him to Christ, for that faith is the gift of God. The faith that Joseph had here, this faith he had when he died, was a faith that he obtained when God visited him in mercy, when God visited him with the Holy Spirit, when God regenerated him by the power of the Holy Ghost, when God effectually called him. When God visited him he was convinced of his sin, he was brought to realise that he was a sinner against God, he was brought to realise that he had a lost and ruined soul, he was brought to realise that he needed to be delivered from the wrath which is to come. He was brought to believe in the New Testament Joseph—his mind was enlightened in the knowledge of Christ, and his will was renewed, so that he embraced Christ in the promise of God as the Christ who was to come. The union between Christ and his soul was effected by faith. That is how we are united to Christ. That is how Joseph was united to Christ. And that faith by which he was united to Christ was the exercise of a living soul by which he touched the hem of Christ's garment—he believed in the Saviour, and he rested in him for eternal salvation. That faith he had when he died.

Once this faith is wrought in the soul of any sinner, it can never be lost. What a consolation that is to the true people of God! Faith may be weak, it may be small. 'Where is your faith?' said the Saviour. 'Why are ye of such little faith?' 'Be not doubtless, but believing,' he said to Thomas. 'O woman, great is thy faith,' he said to another. There may be degrees of faith, there may be little faith and great faith, there may be faith weak in exercise and faith strong in exercise. But one thing we are certain of from the Word of God—faith can never be lost. Sometimes this is a trouble to the people of God. They have hopes that they have faith when they are alive in the world, but they are wondering if they will have faith when they die. Well, you need to have no doubt or fear whatsoever about that. Once faith is wrought in the soul it can never be lost. It may be dim, it may be darkened, it may be weakened, it may be harassed, it may be cast down, but lost it can never be.

Now the next thing we notice is that those who die in the Lord are blessed, not only in the sense that they are united to Christ by faith, and their sins and their iniquities are forgiven, but that their souls are made perfect at death. When Joseph was dying, he was dying in faith that his soul would be prepared to enter eternity. He believed that at death his soul would be made perfect in holiness, and that when he left his body behind he was also leaving sin behind, and leaving sin behind forever. We are told of God's people, 'They shall be brought with gladness great / and mirth on every side, / into the palace of the king / and there they shall abide' (Psalm 45:15). Their souls will be perfect in holiness. Joseph believed that. He believed what Paul said to the church in Philippi—he that began the good work in you shall perform it until the day of Jesus Christ. Until the day of entry into the eternal world, until the day of entry into heaven, the work will be performed—the Holy Spirit will complete it. Their souls shall be completely, wholly, without blemish, without spot, cleansed through the gracious, efficacious power of the Spirit of God. Joseph believed that it would be so when he died.

Also when Joseph died he had no word with regard to the world. He has nothing to say with regard to worldly riches, he is not speaking about any testament or will he has left behind, he is not speaking of the glory that was his in Egypt when he was next to the king. He is not speaking of anything of that nature. He is bidding goodbye to the world and he's bidding goodbye to the world for ever and ever. He is going to heaven, to be with Christ, leaving the world behind. All he's going to leave behind in the world are his bones, and that's all he's concerned about. What a wonderful deathbed this is! Here is a man, a prince in Egypt, a prince in this mighty land, one who had wrought great deliverances for the Egyptians, one who had delivered them from famine, one who had instructed their senators, and now he's bidding goodbye to all that, and all he's talking about is his bones. Nothing about the glory he was leaving behind, nothing about the great works that he did. He was wrapping them all up, casting them all overboard, and going to eternity relying on the blood and righteousness and the grace of Christ. As David Dickson said on his deathbed, 'I have taken all my good deeds, and all my bad deeds, and have cast them together in a heap before the Lord, and have fled from both to Jesus Christ, and in him I have sweet peace.'

Was this not a wonderful way to die, for this wonderful son of God, this pearl, this bright and glorious son among the cedars of Lebanon, among the trees of the wood in the church of God! Now he is to die, now he is going into eternity, and he sees that all these earthly things are fading away as death begins to close his eyes and as his soul turns away from this world and turns to look into the great eternity to which he is going. All he refers to in the world is his bones. What does that demonstrate? Just this, that when he was saying goodbye to the palace of Pharaoh and the riches of Egypt and the unique position of power he had had in the land, he was saying goodbye to them forever, but when he was saying goodbye to his body, he expected to meet his body again. Joseph believed in the resurrection from the dead. He was saying goodbye to these bones, but he believed they were united to Christ as surely as his soul was, and that they would meet him again on the morning of the resurrection. What a wonderful way to die! Saying goodbye to his body and giving charge concerning his bones, in the lively hope and the lively expectation that they would meet again, when time would be no longer, when the palace of Pharaoh would be gone, when the power and glory of Pharaoh would be gone, and the wisdom of his senators lost forever. Joseph believed and hoped and understood that his body would rise again and that his soul, now leaving and going into eternity, would meet with his body again.

In connection with that, he desired that this body would be buried in the land of promise. There is a sense, of course, in which it does not really matter where our bodies are going to be buried. There is a sense in which many have no choice in the matter: they are lost at sea, for instance, and their bodies are never recovered. Perhaps we cannot have our bodies buried where we would desire them to be. Nevertheless one cannot but feel that when Joseph wanted to be buried in the land of promise, it was because he knew all he would ever have in the land or promise was a place where he would be buried. Abraham and Isaac and Jacob had nothing, as far as the land of promise was concerned, but what Abraham called 'a place to bury my dead out of my sight'. Joseph knew very well that that was all he was going to have in the land of promise, and he desired to be buried there. I also feel—although it is just a personal feeling—that he desired to be buried there so that on the resurrection morning, he would rise from the land of promise, and he would rise with Abraham, Isaac and Jacob and all the others who had tasted and seen that God was good. What a wonderful moment that will be on the resurrection morning! Even in this city where you and I live, how many of God's people are buried here! How many of those who suffered for Christ are buried here! In Scotland as a whole, this land for which many desired and prayed that it might be 'thy land, O Immanuel' (Isaiah 8:8), what numbers will rise on the morning of the resurrection!

Joseph wanted to be buried eventually in the Promised Land. The glory of the king, the place where they buried the kings of Egypt, that was not the place for him. No! But to be with Abraham and Isaac and Jacob, to be with those whose dust and whose bones lay in the Promised Land, that's where he wanted to be, even in death.

2. Joseph's faith was in the promise of God

I must go on in the second place to notice Joseph's faith in the promise. He made mention of his bones, the body that he was leaving behind, but he also made mention of the promise of God with regard to his cause in this world. Joseph was leaving the cause of God behind as far as this world was concerned. That cause in which he was such a bright ornament, that cause for which he wrought so wonderful a deliverance at the time of famine, that cause which he was the instrument of preserving in such a wonderful way—he was saying goodbye to it. No longer would they have his prayers; no longer would they have his protection; no longer would they have fellowship and communion with him. He was saying goodbye to the church of God in the world. But as he remembered his own body, so he remembered the body of Christ. He remembered the promise of God with regard to that body, the body of the Saviour, the cause of Christ in the world.

This brings before us that he believed what God had previously revealed, that though the children of Israel were in the land of Egypt now, and although they were now in a state of prosperity there, it was not always to be so. They were to experience bondage, they were to experience tyranny, they were to experience suffering, they were to be under the hand of their taskmasters. They were to be there in such a way that it would seem to them that all the promises of God had failed as far as they were concerned—that Egypt was ruling and Pharaoh was ruling and they were under the hands and power and reign and tyranny of the taskmasters.

Yet Joseph made mention of the departing of the children of Israel. He made mention of their exodus. He made mention of the fact that whatever their troubles and trials and tribulations might be, God would visit them. Whatever their trials and tribulations might be, God was faithful to his promise, and he would never allow anyone to make an end of them. No matter the power of Pharaoh, no matter the power of the taskmaster, God would yet visit them and bring them out of the land of bondage and bring them into the land of promise. Joseph made mention of this when he died. When he was saying goodbye to the church of God in the world, when he was saying goodbye to the sacrifices, when he was saying goodbye to the worship of God there in Goshen, when he was turning his face to eternity, then he remembered his own body, and he also made mention of the body of Christ, the church of God in the world. He assured his brethren that God would surely visit them. The period of trial and temptation and tribulation through which they were to pass did not mean that God had forsaken them. Rather, God was to manifest his glory in a still more glorious way than he had done so far to Abraham, Isaac, Jacob or Joseph himself. In the paschal lamb they were to see a clearer manifestation of the divine Redeemer and of the shelter of the blood and of the salvation of Christ. In the covenant at Mount Sinai they were to see a greater manifestation of the eternal love of God. Yes, at Mount Sinai! We must remember that. True, it was a solemn mount, true, it was a solemn dispensation, but nevertheless it was a dispensation in which God said, 'I am the Lord your God, which brought you out of the land of Egypt, out of the house of bondage.' When Joseph said to his brethren, 'I die, and God will surely visit you, and bring you out of this land into the land which he sware to Abraham, Isaac and Jacob,' this showed his love—his love to Christ's cause, his love to the church of God in the world—and his firm persuasion that despite every trial and tribulation, the promise of God would be fulfilled.

Did not many of the martyrs in Scotland die in this way? Did they not believe that this land of yours and mine, that rests under such a dark cloud of evil and unbelief and apostasy, will yet see days of refreshing and days of reviving? However that may be or whenever that may happen, one thing we know from the Word of God, and that is that there are glorious promises yet to be fulfilled with regard to the church of God in the world. Just now it is passing through a time of tribulation, just now it is oppressed, just now it is ignored, just now it is attacked on the right hand and on the left, but that's not going to change the promise of God. The time is coming when the church will depart out of this time of bondage and time of darkness, into the days of the glorious millennium. We believe that the Word of God teaches plainly that Christ is to reign from the river to the ends of the earth. He will not reign personally, of course. There are people who believe that Christ is coming back to reign on this world again personally. We don't believe that. We believe that Christ will not come back until the resurrection morning, on the day of judgment. But we do believe that through the sceptre of the king of Zion—that is to say, through the gospel of the glory of the blessed God, and by the power of the Holy Spirit—the nations of this world shall become the nations of Christ, in the sense that they shall bow the knee to Zion's king, and the judges and princes of the earth will kiss the Son, and honour and magnify him, not only as king of saints but also king of nations. Despite every tribulation and trial that the church of God may go through now, that glorious time will come. Mr Macfarlane, who was the instrumental cause of preserving the cause of Christ in Scotland among us in 1893, believed that this church to which you and I belong would remain until the days of the millennium, although it may grow small. He quoted these words concerning John the Baptist, 'John did no miracle, but all things John spake of this man are true.' Mr Macfarlane believed that this would be said with regard to this branch of the visible church, that we perform no miracles, but what we are saying about Christ is true! What we are saying about Christ is true, even in a day when his glory and his dignity and his power and his saving love are despised, and when it comes to the day of millennial glory, people will not say anything different about him. You read, if you wish, the revival sermons of George Whitefield, and tell me, or tell anybody, if you hear different from this pulpit. We say the same things, but what is lacking is the power of the Holy Ghost. What is lacking is this, the fulfilment of the promise that God shall visit you!

When Joseph was dying, he mentioned this to his brethren. They had every reason to believe that when Joseph was gone their protection was gone. They had betrayed him, yet they had tasted of his love and his pardon, and he now tells them, as they gather round his bed, 'I die, I leave this world, I am going to eternity,' but he assures them, 'God shall visit you. He shall surely visit you, and bring you into the land of promise, into the land of Abraham, Isaac and Jacob.'

3. Joseph gave commandment concerning his bones

When Joseph spoke this way to the children of Israel, he gave a visible evidence of his faith in the promise of God by giving this commandment concerning his bones, and assuring them that God would visit them. Although two hundred years were to pass before that would happen, he gave this commandment concerning his bones. His remains were not to lie among the kings of Egypt, but they were to be carried out in the exodus. When the children of Israel went out of Egypt through the power of God and by the blood of the paschal lamb, they were to carry the bones of Joseph with them. Therefore they embalmed his body, and left it there as a token that they would not forget Joseph. When they left the land of Egypt, in the midst of all the excitement, in the midst of all the wonder of the deliverance, they would remember Joseph and they would remember the bones of Joseph. And as long as his bones lay there, they were a witness to the fact that God's promise would be fulfilled.

That is what happened. That generation had passed away, but their descendants took Joseph's bones when they left Egypt. Think of Moses the man of God, another bright ornament in the church of God, and a prominent son in the house of God. What an encouragement it must have been to him, when he himself was in Pharaoh's palace, and when he refused to be called the son of Pharaoh's daughter, to remember the bones of Joseph! When he was away yonder forty years in the back of the wilderness around Horeb, as the years were passing and as he was wondering where the deliverance was to come from, surely he would cast his mind back to what Joseph said, and how his bones were to be carried out to the land of promise.

When the time came, Joseph's bones were indeed carried out of Egypt. They were taken to Shechem, in the land of promise, as you may remember from the last verses of the book of Joshua. 'Israel served the Lord all the days of Joshua, and all the days of the elders that out-lived Joshua, that had known all the works of the Lord that he had done for Israel. The bones of Joseph which the children of Israel brought up out of Egypt they buried in Shechem, in a parcel of ground which Jacob bought from the sons of Hamar, the father of Shechem for a hundred pieces of silver, and it became the inheritance of the children of Joseph' (Joshua 24:31–32). Surely that was a wonderful moment in the history of Israel, when the bones of this eminent man of God were brought to rest in this parcel of ground, until they would rise on the morning of the resurrection. In laying them down, the children of Israel knew very well that Joseph had died in faith. He had died in faith of the promises of God for himself, and he died in faith of the promises of God in regard to the cause of God which had been so precious to his soul. Joseph had died in faith, and here it was all fulfilled, as his bones were laid in this parcel of ground, and Israel were in possession of the Promised Land.

It shall also assuredly be fulfilled, with regard no longer to a land, no longer to a spot on God's earth, but with regard to the world at large, that Christ's glory shall spread over it all. His people shall be in every nation and kindred and tongue, and the nations of this world shall become the nations of Christ. The church will see that day. People will see then the value of maintaining the truth of God in the midst of every desolation and persecution and misrepresentation of every description and kind, and they'll see that the promise of God standeth sure. And still later, on the morning of the resurrection, the body of Joseph shall arise from that parcel of ground in Shechem, a body made like unto the body of Christ, and his soul, which has been in heaven now these thousands of years, will then be reunited with the body to which it said goodbye on the bed of death.

O what an extraordinary meeting that shall be! Not only of the body and soul of each individual believer, but all the people of God will meet together on that morning also. The people of God all together, and each one individually, will hear the voice of Christ, saying, 'Come, ye blessed of my Father, and enter the kingdom prepared for you from the foundation of the world.' They shall go in to the marriage supper of the Lamb, together, to be with Christ for ever and ever, and to be enjoying the love of Christ for ever and ever, together. We have no place for the professed grace that has no love to Christ's cause. We don't give any place to pietists, people who have no regard or love to the cause of Christ, and who think they're going to heaven at the same time. Whatever grace they have, it is not the grace Joseph had, and Joseph is in heaven. Whether they are going to be in heaven is another matter altogether. One thing we do know is this, that those who love the promises of God embrace Christ in the promises of God, and they embrace also the people of God in the grace of brotherly love. 'For we know that we have passed from death to life, because we love the brethren.' They shall all be together in the resurrection morning, and they'll all be together throughout the endless ages of eternity, perfectly blessed in the full enjoying of God, world without end.

May he bless his Word.